HOME TRUTHS

AN ANTHOLOGY OF REFUGEE AND
MIGRANT WRITING

HOME TRUTHS

Published in Australia by
Furber
Postal: 7/700 Riversdale Rd, Camberwell, VIC 3124
Tel: +61 414 399 218

First published in Australia 2015
Copyright Furber © 2015
Cover design: Zero21

All rights reserved. No part of this publication may be reproduced, stored in a retrieval system, or transmitted, in any form or by any means without the prior written permission of the publisher, nor be otherwise circulated in any form of binding or cover other than that in which it is published and without a similar condition being imposed on the subsequent purchaser.

National Library of Australia Cataloguing –in –
HOME TRUTHS: AN ANTHOLOGY OF REFUGEE AND MIGRANT WRITING
ISBN: 978-0-9925916-2-5

Cover layout and design by Zero21
Copy and proof edit by Annie Stringer
Original cover image: istock.com/Sergei Dubrovskii
Printed by IngramSpark
Typeset in Palatino 12pt on 12pt

Disclaimer
All care has been taken in the preparation of the information herein, but no responsibility can be accepted by the publisher or author for any damages resulting from the misinterpretation of this work.

HOME TRUTHS

For all who have lost, or found, or are still searching for their home.

All sales profits of this book will be donated to support refugees.

HOME TRUTHS

CONTENTS

JILL PARRIS – Storytelling: An Introduction	1
CAROLINE PETIT & YANNICK THORAVAL – Editors' Note	4
MOHAMED ABBAS OMAR – I Have To Flee	5
CHENAI MUPOTSA – Writing My Life	8
FATEMA JOHERA AHMED – A Suitable Bride	23
BOL – My Story	33
SIDO NDAYI – How I Lost My Eye	48
YING BAI – Happy Kids Harbour	51
HEBA – The Lost Girl	54
KALI PAXINOS – Anguish to Acceptance	61
MOHAMMED ADNAN BHATTI – Letter to Australia	81
ELHAM SHAHHOSEINI – Voiceless Journey	87
YUSUF SHEIKH OMAR – Are We At Peace With Our Names?	95
ESSAN DILERI – A Chapter From Raised in Conflict	102
NIKA SUWARSIH – Move to Melbourne	107
SAEED AFROOZEH – Jay and Black Cloud	115
SARITA KUKLKARNI – Life's Questions, Its Problems & Some Answers	136
WILLIAM DIMO – In Darkness And In Light	146
AJAK KWAI – The Story of Three	177
KALI PAXINOS – I Was A Proxy Bride	183
CLOVIS A. MWAMBA – A Cultural Misunderstanding	188
THE MENTORS	201

STORYTELLING: AN INTRODUCTION

JILL PARRIS

While working as a therapist at the Ecumenical Migration Centre in Melbourne I was asked by a Ugandan man to write his story. After a torturous journey from Uganda to Australia he wanted his neighbours and friends to hear about his life; understand his journey. It was vitally important to him to see his life written down. He said that counselling had helped him settle in Australia, but had not helped the wider Australian community to accept him for who he was. He hoped writing his story down would.

For two decades he survived grinding poverty, stood up for his neighbours in the face of many avenging dictatorships and stayed alive in the face of corrupt governments that sought his death. Somehow was able to maintain a sense of justice throughout.

As a refugee from South Africa, I know how important it is to feel accepted in a new land where you have no connection. This brave Ugandan man, with his pain and estrangement, reminded me of my own overwhelming ache to belong. It is something I can taste and feel to this day.

I remember settling into our new Australian house and going food shopping for my family for the first time. In the checkout queue I fell to the floor, burst into tears and wept uncontrollably because I could not find Joko tea. Ridiculous! It took ages to feel Australian. After thirty-five years, there are still times I long for home.

For me, writing helps capture significant experiences that have shaped who I am and invites others to understand me. When memories are traumatic, the writing process helps me become more objective and gain some distance from a tsunami of bewildering feelings. Knowing that others will read about what has happened to me helps validate my hurt.

Many others at the Centre approached me about writing their stories and I sought help. I asked Writers' Victoria for support. Writers' Victoria loved the idea of working with refugees and secured money from the Melbourne Lord Mayor's Fund. We formed a group of storywriters who met at the Wheeler Centre and were taught for a season by renowned author Robert Hillman. Working with Robert was inspiring and our stories developed.

During this time we refugees and migrants began talking about the importance of sharing our stories. We wanted to introduce our fellow Australians to our home countries; we wanted them to understand how and why we had to flee to this distant country and why we needed their goodwill to flourish in our new homes.

As the politics of settlement in Australia became more fraught, I wanted our stories to be heard. Only, like many good and just things, money for a facilitator/teacher ran out. Yet our enthusiasm continued. So I recruited thirteen members of Writers' Victoria as mentors and paired one with each storyteller. The process of stabilising mentorship pairs was slow and sometimes fraught, but this unique arrangement has allowed for sustained writing support of the storyteller. Coming together on a monthly basis built respect and generated a democratic group process. The one to one mentorships have helped many writers sharpen their skills, built respectful relationships and generated this anthology.

Writers have brought not only their unique tales born out of extraordinary lives and journeys, but also their cultural storytelling traditions, humour and history. Mentors have pooled their wealth of knowledge about collecting, crafting, writing, editing and presenting work to an Australian audience. I thank them all.

Together we have produced this book *Home Truths: An Anthology Of Refugee And Migrant Writing* - a diverse anthology that we proudly offer for your reading pleasure.

With love, expectation and hope

Jill Parris

EDITORS' NOTE

Home Truths: An Anthology Of Refugee And Migrant Writing is a collection of stories, essays and poems written by a diverse group of writers, mostly from Africa and Asia. The anthology is filled with first hand experiences of war and dislocation, and of being at odds with one's own culture.

We have been privileged to edit *Home Truths* and have tried to honour each author's voice. Some authors are skilled writers who had little or no need of mentors; their work required little editing. Others found the process of writing their stories and experiences difficult, even with the guidance of mentors. We recognise that it is difficult to transform personal – often traumatic – experiences and feelings into smooth story telling. These are the words as the authors chose to share them.

For some writers, English is their third or fourth language and writing in English is a struggle. As editors, we tried to preserve this raw quality of some of the writing because it underlines the author's need to overcome cultural and linguistic barriers to tell their story. Demonstrating a universal will to connect and build relationships is one of this book's ambitions.

Some writers originate from countries with an oral tradition where stories have their own internal structures and conventions. We have tried to honour these traditions while adhering to the structural conventions of the English language. In our editing, we aimed to strike a balance between the writer's need to be heard and the reader's need to understand.

Caroline Petit & Yannick Thoraval

I HAVE TO FLEE

MOHAMED ABBAS OMAR

The night before my whole life changed I went to bed earlier than usual. I wanted to be well rested and alert for my first day at university, but I was so excited I couldn't fall asleep immediately.

I had slept only a few hours when I was shocked awake by a massive explosion. This is how Somalia's citizens learned civil war had broken out in the city of Mogadishu. Artillery shells pounded buildings and bullets strafed the population like lethal metal rain.

It was beautiful weather in Mogadishu—the sky blue and cloudless and only seven-thirty in the morning, when my father and I heard another blast coming from the direction we were heading in. It was slightly to the right of the university I planned to enrol in. We hardly had time to think what this meant when we heard someone with a loud speaker shouting, 'War'.

My father is not a fortune-teller but he has an acute sixth sense about many things. A long time ago my dad understood that someday there would be a civil war in Somalia.

After the explosion my father turned the car around to head back to where we had come from, but we were stopped by the only traffic light still functioning in the Somali capital. We waited for the green light to come after the yellow; instead the light was red again.

'Why has light turned red faster than usual dad?' I asked.

'Maybe the traffic light is a warning. It may be a message that Somalia is marching into total collapse and people should flee all the faster' dad replied.

Suddenly there were two armed men in civilian clothes standing before us. We thought they must be undercover police securing the city—but we were wrong. The gunmen demanded my father hand over his car keys.

From their accent we realised these men were members of the militia clan, who under cover of darkness had entered our sleeping city in secret to overthrow the unelected military government.

The day was hot now and we were right in the heart of Mogadishu. We walked back to our house in a state of shock, feeling like our bodies had become too heavy for our bones to carry. From that day on our lives were never the same again.

Wise men say there is no permanent condition in life. Life changes like the wind, sometimes bringing good news and other times bad. I recall my grandmother saying one should always be ready for anything because a pot of honey cannot last forever.

Our people were united, living peacefully side-by-side, until the warlords came. They destroyed our harmonious co-existence. Mogadishu was a blessed and peaceful city that enjoyed the title 'Pearl of the Indian Ocean', but when bullets rained down on us I had no place to hide.

I left my beloved city; I left my country, my school and my friends. I ran for my life and spent my most of my teenage years on the run, not knowing where I would end up. From exile I wondered if the smiling faces of my school friends were still there in Mogadishu. Are they still alive, wondering why I abandoned them? Have I betrayed them in some way?

Every day I wonder if I will ever see my childhood friends again. For myself, my dream of becoming a university student proved to be as difficult as putting a man on the moon after that terrible last day when I left my home and all that I had known before so far behind me.

About The Author

Dr Mohamed Abbas Omar, PhD was born in Somalia. In his late teens, with only one year left to finish high school he fled with his family from Mogadishu after the central government was overthrown by armed militia. Later he was granted a scholarship by the Malaysian government to study Islamic Studies and Political Science. In 2010 he earned his PhD on war and peace studies from the International Islamic University of Malaysia (IIUM).

Dr Mohamed moved to Australia in 2011 and started voluntary work in Melbourne as an English teacher assisting newly arrived migrants and refugees from the East African community. He has also worked as an Assistant Researcher at the National Centre of Excellence for Islamic Studies at the University of Melbourne.

Dr Mohamed's passion for writing and literature started after he read Sweet and Sour Milk, a novel written by Nuruddin Farah, Somalia's international literary icon who has been shortlisted for the Nobel Prize in Literature many times. Dr Mohamed was also influenced by other writers such as Chinua Achebe, Wole Soyinka, Ngugi Wa Thiong'o, Alice Munro, Toni Morrison and Isabel Allende.

Dr Mohamed Abbas contributes to public debate on various issues through articles published in academic journals, websites and newspapers. He speaks fluent English and Arabic and Bahasa Malaysia at a conversational level. He is married with two sons.

WRITING MY LIFE

CHENAI MUPOTSA

My house my life

I am a house; we are all houses. Some houses have perfectly manicured lawns, flowerbeds full of love and colour, with bees dancing on top of the flowers. They are perfectly painted; when you look into the window you see just enough to know this is truly a nice house. But perfection is an illusion. I think my house is nice on the outside. I think it's vibrant and colourful, and gives the promise of endless comfort and bliss. But outsides are outsides; we don't always know what awaits us inside. My house is a work in progress. There is more perfection on the outside than within. Superficially all looks well, yet this changes every day. My house, like a real house, needs work: the pipes spring a leak, the walls need regular repainting, at times there is a termite infestation or mice pay a visit. The work you need to do on a house never ends. It will never end. But it's a wonderful feeling to know you will never reach perfection. The work is continual, but therapeutic. So I tend to my house, I love my house with all its imperfections. I tend to my house by writing and feeling love through it all; whether it is joy, or pain, it's okay and all is well.

The sky inside me

I feel a sky inside of me, much like the one on the exterior of my being, up above. Some days there are clear blue skies, it's sunny—on these days I move through life uninhibited, free from the burden of obstructions. The clarity within me allows for clarity in the world—I see beauty, I feel laughter well up inside and escape out my mouth, I see lips moving on people's faces and myself receiving these words and returning my own musings—I am a part of it. Occasionally a negative thought wafts by, like a cirrus cloud in my mind, but it's mostly sunny and I am one with the world. And as the day draws to a close and nightfall hits my little world, I lay my head with thoughts that send me off to the twinkling stars of my clear sky.

Then at times it's partially cloudy. That's okay: clouds vary in size, density, shape and colour. The joy of it being partially cloudy is the ability to still have the clarity of the sky. So a feeling of panic and dread comes along disguised as a nimbostratus cloud in the sky of my soul. It hides the sun and the mood changes. Feelings take over as the cloud covers the sun. But with the sanity granted by the magical blue daylight, I can see it is just a cloud and watch it come and go. My outer being breathes while my inner self understands feelings come and go. It goes and the sunshine is restored.

Alas there are times when it is overcast: cumulonimbus clouds haunt my sky or stratus clouds prance with the threat of drizzle. The sky is covered and it is grey, as am I. There is no reasoning without the clarity of the sky and the anchor of sanity it provides. One cannot watch clouds come and go when all there is, is clouds—it's as if they remain still and constant, as if all there will ever be is clouds, all there will ever be is greyness—and the world is nothing but sadness. Each cloud is a thought or fear or memory. They well up together, creating chaos in the sky, crippling the outer me. A storm brews as the rain falls; tears run down my face and in this moment I can't imagine the sky will ever be blue again. I imagine all I will ever feel is pain, loneliness, inadequacy, fear, dread and dismay; so overwhelming they form an accumulation of clouds so strong the weight is too much to hold. On the ground I lie in the same position as I lay in my mother's womb, clinging to my chest. I feel each lightning bolt hit, the thunderclap, each jolt a physical pain in my chest. As I drift off into the darkness all I hope for is that the clouds clear the next day.

Hypnotherapist visit

I'm sitting in my car, heart racing, wondering what on earth I am doing? A hypnotherapist...really Chenai? Breathe in...breathe out. I notice dried up yogurt on the floor of my car, the dried up old banana peel on my seat. Oh there's also an apple core that's moved past oxidisation and is venturing into mouldy territory. Worst case scenario this guy can make me less gross; because my car is like a rubbish bin, all its contents, myself included. Before I step out of the car I check my lip gloss, make sure I don't have panda eye, okay all good. I step out to hear the click-clacking of my heels on the pavement. I wonder if any of these people know what a fraud I am—pretending to be put together and shiny, eyes bright, smile on my face, specially selected outfit placed on my body with care, and appropriately accessorised—when really what lives inside me is fear, anxiety and an indescribable darkness I often get lost in, drown in, only to have my body float to the surface lifeless days after, needing resuscitation.

I am at the door, last chance to run away. No, I am going in. My heart is beating so fast I think it might be to the rhythm of an eerie song yet to be written. My heart wants to escape from my chest and come out of my mouth, my blood is racing around my body as if there is a tsunami in my veins. Am I dying? I may be dying? But I am nearly dying a lot so I think I will be all right. Knock, knock ...here we go. I enter, smelling incense, and there is a tiny little man who looks like Ghandi. I don't know what it felt like to be around Ghandi but I am pretty sure this is it. My heart slows, my mind calms and my mouth gets ready to unleash. I am safe. I have a weird feeling that something magical may be about to happen.

He seems to know about me before I tell him anything; either I am predictable, typical, just another jaded broken soul...or... he's a witch. There's something strange about this little man. I'm going with witch for now—no, wizard. Then he surprises me, he says something that brings me to tears, uncontrollable tears. He's talking about her, the little girl inside me, little me, and why it is she's so little and fragile and still inside me. I no longer care whether I'm seen through, or if he is a sort of warlock. He tells me time does not exist for me now, me as a child and me in the future all exist all at once. He tells me my best role model now is myself in the future and the best person to console the broken little girl is me now. I can tell her it's fine and I am okay.

How could I face her? I felt so guilty and ashamed. There's nothing I could've done because I am her, but still I let us down, all of us, every form, age and stage of me. That's why I'm lying here still broken: I failed us. I'm not who any of them imagined I would be, I've become weaker, more frightened, fear has me in its grip and I'm not sure I will ever be free.

It's time now, we have arrived, here she is: 'little Chen-Chen'. I hug her and start to weep. Little me weeps, the me visiting her weeps and my limp body lying in the hypnotherapist's chair weeps. Crouched down at eye level with little Chen-Chen I tell her how so very sorry I am she is alone and sad. I hear a voice tell me to tell her it will be okay. I hesitate, but will it really? Have you watched the news I think? I don't want to lie to her. I say it anyway: 'Everything is going to be okay little one, I promise, I'm you from the future and I'm here to tell you, you grow up and the world makes a bit more sense each day and you get less terrified every day until one day there is just a trickle of fear, it no longer rules us.'

I hold Chen-Chen close and tears fall down my hypnotised body's face, they fall and fall. I lie still, unable to wipe my tears. I feel my heart cry out, the pain is unbearable. I hold this little girl and I say goodbye to everything I wish she'd been, for she is who she is and I am who I am because of it. I can't let her go. She's so little and so alone, the worries of someone ten times her age, the face of a mischievous little munchkin and a heart so hardened in a mere four years of living. I hold her and repeat over and over that she need not worry.

I need more time with her but I hear Jean-Alain guiding me to the next part of me that needs a hug. He says, 'Now put her somewhere safe in your heart where she can play, worry free'. I know exactly where to put her: I picked her up and visualised walking her into my heart and I felt the pain melt as I turned on a light switch, a light switch so magnificent it had the power to turn on the sun. Grass grew beneath our feet and suddenly we were in a garden, my back garden where I should have played carefree but didn't, couldn't. I turned on the sprinklers and using my new found magic put little me in a pink frilly swimsuit. 'Play in the sprinklers my love, laugh, and be merry, you are so, so loved and you are okay.' I felt the burden of a thousand broken promises lift from her tiny body as she began to frolic in the sprinklers, laughing, looking very much like the four year old I'd always wished I'd gotten to be. The past ceased to matter then. All that mattered was for now and the rest of my days little Chen-Chen would get to live the life I wanted for her; playing worry free in the sprinklers inside my heart.

I found a new freedom in that office, a new energy, a new strength and acceptance of all that had been and would be. For the first time the fire was burning in my heart, not on my face, not in my eyes. It was a brilliant, dazzling fire dancing around to the tune of a happy song. It was contrasted by the cold on my face and fingers as I walked rapidly that cold Melbourne winter morning. I could feel my heart pumping every ounce of blood through my body, the mechanics felt effortless yet real as I felt every part of my body work in unison. I wanted to scream, 'I'm alive!' I'd never felt so alive. Twenty-eight years of living and I finally knew what it meant to live, to be a part of, to participate in the complex dance that is life. I noticed the flowers blooming and the awe of their beauty and the annoyance at myself for not knowing the name of each flower, all outweighed by the thrill of being in the moment. In the moment I noticed the grass growing between the cracks in the concrete. I noticed the old trees with their withered bark telling a tale as wrinkles do in a face. I noticed the people I walked past, I made eye contact and smiled. Warmth filled my heart when they smiled back and there it was…connection. The thing I had never known but that was now my companion, my drug, my reason for being. To see and to be seen, to hear and to be heard, to join my world with that of others. It was a magic I'd lived far too long without and would never be without again. It was as if the world was made with me in mind, so I could absorb it, inhale it, appreciate it in every way possible, but until now I hadn't noticed. I would look, feel and listen twice as long and twice as hard to make up for it. Every chubby baby I saw my heart would soften for, as if I had seen two of them, even three. There was no limit to my capacity to feel for and with others. The wound had healed, the scar tissue dropped off, leaving a resilient human being who was just ready, ready for…whatever was coming next.

My mess
My sheets tell a tale…

My first encounter is with an unpopped kernel of popcorn.
The sight of it brings forth memories of its deliciousness
And the discomfort it and its friends brought to me in my sleep.

Why are there so many hair ties? Each a broken promise,
An unfulfilled intention to keep my braids at bay as I slumber.
But instead another obstruction as I toss and turn.

The empty snack packets represent my routine mindless scoffing
To silence the growling wolf that howls from my stomach.
Satisfied briefly it dozes, then awakens at the thought of further appeasement.
With all the crumbs, packets and even post-it notes, I find

A throng of multivitamins, strewn throughout my bedding haphazardly,
As each moment passes each tiny bundle becomes less nutritious
Leaving but an oxidised mound, a deterrent to sleep.

With all this knowledge and a brand new day I must decide the fate of my bed mates

I cover them gently with my doona, which tells a lie that a normal bed lies beneath,

Tonight my pretties…I shall encounter you again,

Feel your disruptions, contemplate change and respread you tomorrow.

Some Of My Loves
Jack the Kitten
I hear a little rumble, rumble, rumble
And feel the vibrations of each rippling movement
His little warm belly moves up and down
And I know he is happy, so I am happy.

The magical purrs of a happy kitten
Rumbling on my lap
Rumble, rumble, rumble.

May this kitten purring never end
All is right in the world
When I hear the rumbles of my furry friend.

Lidia
When she smiles her eyes sparkle,
With the whimsy of the glistening sea,
And when she laughs it's super loud,
It warms me from within.

Those ocean eyes are full of kindness,
A tiny hint of what her soul beholds.
Your life, your heart will never be the same,
Once you meet this character so bold.

Her golden skin and wondrous face her beauty is alluring,
It's only but the surface of all her hidden wonder.

So on this late December night,
I thank my lucky stars,
For this sweet angel who makes my world so bright.

'Tis my birthday wish for you my gorgeous friend
That you see your majesty and how you make the world so great.

Charlie

Lights dance on the edges of his curls, each bump, swirl and sweep is perfectly framed with a luminescent glow. Is it a halo generated by inner peace, joy and acceptance flowing abundantly through this gentle soul? I stare perplexed; my stare is caught and met with a smile. Each tooth is perfectly in place as only an orthodontist could have orchestrated. With a dimple on either side, signifying it was face designed to smile with consistency and effortlessness. At times my lips quiver as I smile, they quiver in rebellion, the muscles protesting the fraud my face perpetrates. I smile awkwardly and my lips tremble, mimicking the beat at which my heart races; my body lacks unison as my visible self attempts to falsify the look of ease and contentment. How is it that this haloed man has so much light where my darkness lives, almost as if I was born in an empty cave and he an open garden bursting with colour and life? How do I turn on the light in my cave and allow a garden to grow, so I too can instinctively have my lips curl with joy, I too can be a fluorescent light and I too can live in day and not night?

HOME TRUTHS

Mummy
I dream of your cheeky smiley face,
The calming presence of your space.

I think of drowning in a hug,
And cuddling up in a ball so snug.

You make me laugh, you make me smile.
I don't even notice it's been a while.

It's afternoon and we are still in our pyjamas,
Laughing at a television drama.

I store up every single little word,
All the wisdom and even the absurd.

I carry you around, you are a part of me,
For you my love is infinite, like the sea.
So my beautiful, precious mother,
Always know, like you, there is no other.

Hope
The end of a workday,
This is the sight of the end of a day,
A vision of all we were and all we will be again

When we hop back on the mechanical serpent
And ride her towards that view
Where people are clothed in black
And walk with haste
Adorned with masks to hide their face.

Alone we all walk surrounded by many,
Until we can return to safety,
Riding away from that view.

HOME TRUTHS

Promises
Peeking out from behind the trees is a promise,
A promise of hope, a promise pain will go,
A promise I need never be alone.

From when I emerge from the Underground,
The day's hopes fresh in my eyes for all at Parliament Station to see,
To when I return down Brunswick Street at the day's end,
Triumphant in the glow of survival,
There I see my pyramid of hope.

Its backdrop differs but its form remains resolute,
A never changing promise.

As long as I see it I know all is well.
I know there is a place where my knees can touch the ground,
Tears can flow uninhibited down my face,
And every fear I have ever felt can be brought forward
And I am heard, I am soothed, I am loved and…I am fine.

So I feel hope every time I see this promise
Dancing in sync with my stride between the buildings,
Playing coyly behind the greenery
And making its glorious presence known to each passing tram.

My sweet promise, your site takes with it tiny quivers of anxiety,
Sucks up the tiny bits of darkness which threaten to multiply and take hold,
And leaves room for light to shine
And for all your promises of hope to fill my soul.

Despair

In my chest sits this tight ball; it interferes with my heartbeat and alters my breath. It lingers there, an unwanted squatter chipping away at my joy and leaving a hollowed out crevasse where my peace once rested. Why is it just a few words bring forth a tsunami of memories? Each memory so vivid it's as if they are all relived within that moment. Each bit of hurt promptly followed by anger, the anger illuminated by a feeling of injustice. The hurt and the anger join forces, further tightening my chest and weakening my body. It's as if I stood below a tree from which a beehive dropped, the bees are frantically buzzing about stinging without warning. Real life bee stings may leave inflammation and physical pain but the buzzing bees in my mind don't die once they've stung, they continue to frantically race about. I cannot see what's in front of me, all there is is the berserk chaos of a thousand tiny stinging creatures, each a powerful painful thought and together resulting in an emotional anaphylactic shock. How is it that another is permitted to cause so much chaos, to unleash bees in my mind and chip away at my heart, to even suck the light from my soul? Leave my being in a state of de-synchronisation? Suddenly I lose control of my thoughts, emotions even the command of my limbs, and I am frozen. My body is frozen and I am in the sea and I wonder how I will ever get to shore. How I will ever get control of all that I think and feel—and in that moment it's as if I never will again—I shall cling to my life raft of hope as I am stranded in the sea with my bee filled head and hollow heart.

Consoled

As I wept deeply, eyes red, face hot, mucus dribbling from my nose, I felt these arms around me. 'It's okay', I heard in a male voice. It was as if God had unleashed a flood that could be likened only to the one which Noah and his ark survived. Confusion, tension, worry and warmth all formed the waters underneath which my ark of pain floated. How was it that male arms could hold me, that I could feel the firmness of this chest and hear this voice but not have my entire body, shriek, rebel, be filled with fear and then run? Who was this magical man who kept away my fear and revulsion and allowed my body, along with all its fears, hurt and worry, to melt into this hug, and my pain to flow without the usual protective dam preventing any and all movement? As I felt this touch I realised I had never known a touch like this, one which came from a male but came with innocence, safety and security. As I heard that it was okay I realised it was, then also realised all the times it hadn't been okay and this saddened me deeper. More tears ran down my face and I felt my heart start to vomit, as if it were a stomach that had eaten something bad. And I felt my heart purge the bad, felt it choose to throw away the bad memories of the past and hold onto this new idea, that it is okay, that I was safe, that I need not fear touch or comfort, that I need not travel through this world alone. This large organ that is my skin need no longer hide away from its fellows, it needn't raise every hair on it at the thought of closeness, or cause the muscles it covered to seize. It needed simple words soaked in 'It's okay', to allow the hand which rubbed my back to do its job and console.

The twins

It's 1990 and two little girls are playing outside. They look exactly the same, speak the same, have the same untameable Afro hair rivalled only by the stubbornness of their little spirits. These little beings have lived the same life, had all the same experiences, received the same amount of love and affection, yet they are different. One is Light, she shines bright with an inner warmth, glow and peace. The other is Darkness, a permanent shadow cast upon her skinny frame, the weight of the world on her shoulders and more sorrow than she could've possibly seen in her five years of being alive living in her heart. Little Light plays fearlessly, loves boldly and sees the beauty in everything. She was once hospitalised for having eaten a flower she deemed so beautiful it needed to become a part of her, the only way she knew to do this was to consume it. Darkness acted like the weight bringing Light back down to earth: 'Don't go over there something bad will happen. Don't talk to those children they already hate us, I can feel it from here.' And the constant mantra: 'We aren't good enough for that, to eat that, play with that, talk to them or do that, we belong alone just the two of us.' Light listened. She took on the words of Darkness as if they were a suit of armour. But a bit of her light still shone out of the cracks, she hoped one day to be strong enough to be the dominant one. Darkness was both her captor and her saviour. Darkness kept her locked in a life different from the one she felt was meant for her, but saved her from all the things there were to fear. She need never worry: Darkness did all the worry. Yet she hoped one day to walk hand in hand with Darkness—lit up, connecting with the world, not fearing the world, seeing every person as an opportunity for shared laughter; every cloud as a magical, dancing, floaty figure; every tree as life giving and beautiful and every day as an adventure to be explored. One day Light would win but for now Darkness was in charge. So we find on this warm day in 1990, Light and Dark playing outside just the two of them their dog and their cat, both animals with black shiny coats as dark as Darkness believes her soul to be. The four sit outside eating dog food away from the rest of the children. *One day....* thinks Light, seeing what freedom, innocence and joy look like on the face of a child running through the sprinklers, *'one day Darkness will change or go away and I will play like a real little girl.'*

Love
My heart is bursting with love,
Each one of its beats is like the thump of a drum.

Air dances across my rib cage as if it were a xylophone,
And then exits my nostrils with the whistle of a flute.

My body makes the soundtrack for my love,
The garden of love that grows inside it,
Seeds planted by God,
Fertilised by the love of others,
And cultivated by the goodness of the world.

My heart is bursting with love,
May the pollen I have been gifted spread,
So many gardens of love may grow,
And we can all be bursting with love.

The End
There is no end; this is just the beginning. I am on the road and will never stop travelling. There are potholes, bumps, rough terrain, dirt roads—but the scenery is always beautiful. When the road is smooth, I can enjoy my surroundings and the things and people I pass on my journey. Thank you for peeking into a little part of my travels.

About The Author

On the 25th of January 1985, the universe selected my father's most sprightly sperm for the honour of fertilising its carefully chosen ovum counterpart. Together they created a little zygote in which my soul was able to enter and the journey of Chenai Mupotsa began. Nine months later I was born in Harare, Zimbabwe. I wanted to stay in the womb, but I had to deal with my ejection. I did so with humour and imagination. I lived a pretty eventful life with imaginary friends, travel, adventure, multiple injuries, a love for sugar, an all-girls Anglican School education and more detentions than I would like to remember. I wrote, I painted, I danced and I also wept at times. Fast forward a further 17 years, and I made it through the tough regiment of my structured adolescence and got to enjoy the fruits of my labour, having made it into university in Australia. Thus began a new journey: a rebirth, an adaptation into a new existence, and an amalgamation of the Chenai I thought I needed to be and the one I actually was. It was the start of the internal dialogue of my personal Home Truths. A tiny bit of which I have the privilege of sharing in this forum, I hope you relate, engage, connect and are inspired.

A SUITABLE BRIDE

FATEMA JOHERA AHMED

It was going to be the last time, Orni promised herself. After that, it didn't matter what they said. She was going to refuse. Thirty-two in Bangladesh, Orni was obliged to marry whatever came her way. With Aunty Reeha as chaperone, Orni obeyed. Sightings with potential in-laws were exhausting. They called it sari shopping, but the mall was only a pretext to the mission. Orni was the one on sale, and she was going to be handed to any fool who could be convinced she was a good buy.

It was not Orni's first exhibition. Aunty Reeha ceaselessly reminded her to stay away from the expensive saris; they insinuated Orni was high maintenance. Everyone wanted a simple, malleable girl they could dress up or strip down. Orni was miserable every time she had appointments at the mall. Each trip made her feel a failure. She felt less human until she identified more with the saris on discount because they too had faults. Orni stared at the passers-by. She hoped for some flicker of recognition, even of the human urge in others to acquire things and wives. No one returned her gaze. Aunty Reeha saw her and scolded Orni until she was as still as the mannequins.

"It will break your Ma's heart if your tantrums disappoint her again. I will give her an unbiased report," Aunty Reeha said.

"I'm just so nervous," Orni said.

"This could be your last chance."

"I wish you weren't so blunt."

Aunty Reeha was right. She was in the way. Proposals were coming in for her twenty-five year old sister.

There was a soothing quality about Aunty Reeha that Orni's

Ma had not inherited. Ma was petulant when her ideas held her, and lacked subtlety when it came to Orni's husband issues. Aunty Reeha earned her place as an expert matchmaker having gotten her four daughters off her hands despite being widowed. Her steady, dyed black head, two steps ahead of her counterparts, silenced Orni's objections. Aunty Reeha yielded the maternal to draw young people to her; they soon dropped like exhausted moths tinged with overexposure. People like Aunty Reeha were dangerous, Orni decided.

"Look happy until further instructions," Aunty Reeha chirped as Orni walked to her usual corner.

"Why don't you talk to me?"

"We don't want to appear as two chatterboxes. Where's the dignity in that?"

Orni's days were numbered. She had enchantments to perform. Soon the floodgates would crash, and Orni's eligibility would draw widowers and divorced men. Only desperate women married desperate men. What would the neighbours say?

Yet she was already a transgressor. Her laughs were ceaseless giggles, morally unsound; her confident stride, the prancing of a loose woman, out of control; the careless toss of hair away from her round face, the call for rescue from a life without love. Everything gave offence. Orni needed to be curtailed. Marriage and a man would take care of it. Not an impossible, Herculean task if her parents were respectable.

The instructions were not new. Orni stirred their vague implications in the cauldron of dos and don'ts. She concocted a cankerous liquid it would be death to drink. She was being set up. There was no want of feedback too: she was too chirpy, too edgy or too disinterested; she was too short or her heels were too pretentiously high; she laughed when she was to respond or responded when it was better to be silent. It was endlessly contradictory until Orni chose the easiest way – becoming the embodiment of Bengali womanhood who was not seen, and not heard, and had not been.

She felt the piercing eyes of her evaluators as they casually undressed and appraised her form for defects like one pressed a tomato. The careless examination only imprinted the depreciating fruit, made it worse for wear for the next wandering, uninformed hand. She was nearing expiry though the life expectancy estimated seventy years of misery for the average Bangladeshi middle-class woman. Her voluptuousness stuck to her like black mould to an aging tomato. "Only the best for the tomato soup I'm making my son," the white-haired, stooping figure of her imaginary mother-in-law squealed in the kitchen, a knife in her hand ready to stab lovingly away at the ingredients of the day. It did not matter her son did not want soup.

Orni felt a second violation of her body as the careless hand tossed the tomato back into the rejected pile. She was disoriented by the tumble and the halting thud as she grappled with what she was – a thirty-two year old, displayed at the mall to marry; a thirty-two year old reluctant to be rescued, driven insane by rejection. These moments undid Orni. They shredded everything by which she defined herself. Orni focused on the nondescript back of the passing heads. The anonymity reminded her it did not matter what she thought. Unlike herself, family honour was perennial and really existed.

"Stop looking like you're having a terrible time," Aunty Reeha screeched as she pinched Orni's arm.

Aunty Reeha rubbed the beady pearls of perspiration that formed on her upper lip. The moist tissue was worn out, coming apart, and tiny bits stuck to her face. She looked comical. Orni picked off the pieces one by one. Aunty Reeha was human, just like her.

"Why don't they meet me in person?"

"What do you think they are doing? Quiz them all you like when you're married to them."

Orni knew she could not dictate terms: she was lucky she had a meeting to attend. The family coming to the mall wanted to appraise her physical suitability with their son. They wanted only to watch her in a natural environment. Orni's task was to pretend she was unaware of their presence and intentions. She needed to gain their approval by being herself. But Orni could not acquiesce to the mall being a natural habitat. Nor did she understand how to pose to gain their acceptance. It was incredible, but still happened to women in some form or other.

Orni frowned as Aunty Reeha reached into her handbag for her cell phone the umpteenth time. The screen lit up almost in response and the phone vibrated. Aunty Reeha answered immediately. Instinct told Orni the call concerned her. Time stopped as she waited. Would there be further instructions? What more could be demanded that she did not want to give?

Aunty Reeha spoke graciously even as she shouted into the mouthpiece: they were grateful to be considered; inconveniences were apologised for; further requests were invited – pleaded for; she hoped to hear from them soon; the blessings of the divine and the influence of predestination in these matters were remembered; goodbyes were said; the name of the most Gracious, most Merciful was hailed, His pleasure invoked. Aunty Reeha waited quietly for Orni's potential benefactors to disconnect before replacing the phone. The exhibition had ended. It was time to go home.

The day weighed heavily on Orni as she trudged towards the exit. She felt she had not done enough. What if more could be done, but she had been too wilful? Orni no longer sought happiness in marriage. For her, it was redemption. She glanced at her watch. They had been loitering twenty minutes. It always ended quickly.

"The surest way to marry is to go with the flow," Aunty Reeha announced to her sister as Ma opened the door.

"We've been duelling," Ma said.

"Baba is right to suspect. I don't like the way they speak to us like they're doing us a favour," Orni said.

"A groom's family will want the upper hand and the bride's family placates. It's culture," Aunty Reeha said.

"Everything's culture, and nothing's common sense," Orni said.

HOME TRUTHS

The banter with Aunty Reeha and Ma was ceaseless. They never agreed. Orni was alone in her anger. Yet the proposal disturbed everyone. The groom's family outraged even the hardcore cultural adherents in Orni's family. Reports came from indignant sources. Orni's employer was asked if she was flighty. Orni's sister was investigated for similar charges. Calls were made to the extended family about their financial stability. They wanted to know if Orni's family was respectable, the qualifications of her parents, and their ancestral integrity up to three generations. Talks were initiated about gifting Shovon, the groom, a car if all went well. Ma remained hopeful of a change in their goodwill once the match was approved; maybe the car could be negotiated into a television. Baba trudged along.

"Orni's Baba and I were looking into our loan options. We could have married Orni off long ago instead of knit-picking all the suitors you sent over the years! The demands would have been less too if Orni was younger," Ma said.

"Tell them we believe in simple Islamic weddings," Orni said.

"Austerity is not done. Everyone would feel cheated of their share of festivity with a simple 'I do' if you distribute only cheap dates among guests," Aunty Reeha said.

They joined Baba at the dining table.

"Things will move very fast," Aunty Reeha announced.

Orni felt the thinness of Aunty Reeha's reassurances. Even if a proposal was made to Orni, she foresaw a life of giving in for herself and her family. What if Shovon's family never came to see them as equals? What if the insolence of a week became the humiliation of a lifetime? These were gruelling questions with unsatisfactory answers.

"Where's the festivity if it's going to break our backs to meet the expenses?" Orni said.

"Did Shovon speak with you at the sighting?" Baba said.

"Thankfully they called asking us to leave. Or we would have been stranded there indefinitely," Orni shrugged.

"They don't believe in the bride and groom meeting.

They only wanted to see if Orni looked older than her age," Aunty Reeha said.

Orni saw Baba wince. She saw how much the stench of her decay had already travelled into the sanctity of her family, her last stand against the world.

"Traditional families have a propensity to marry without second thoughts. Where's the guarantee you will find someone better if you delay talks with this family? When was the last time you brought in a proposal? Think of what another postponement will reduce Orni to," Aunty Reeha said.

"We have to think of Shorna as well. She's going to be twenty-six this year. How long will her fiancé's family wait? Maybe they are looking already given the window of opportunity our requests for time to deal with Orni's problem has gifted them,' Ma said. "We've raised our daughters with the lesson of patience. Orni has the fortitude to make every circumstance her own. Shovon is an only child. Orni will thrive once she learns their ways. What will happen to Shorna if her future in-laws change their mind? Everyone knows about her engagement. It's social suicide."

"Go ahead with Shorna's wedding. I'll wait rather than have the family sunk in debt and unhealthy relations," Orni said.

"And will you be absent from the wedding too? Think of the questions we will be asked. Think of Shorna's own place, the questions she will be asked by her in-laws. Her humiliation," Aunty Reeha said. "Shovon's family seems different. They are traditional, yes. But they want an educated, working woman. You will continue teaching. They are not after a domesticated woman they can dictate terms to."

"These days a working woman is sought to contribute to the in-law's household, not because she is a catch," Orni ventured.

"I don't want to hear another objection from you," Ma said. She turned to Baba, "Don't you like Shovon?"

"I met him at his workplace during his lunch hour. He looked at least five years older than the photograph *his* family sent. He was busy and couldn't talk much."

"Enough to know he has a demanding, respectable job. His bio data is fact-checked. Look at the facts: he comes from a traditional family. He does as he is told. When his Ma asked if he had any preferences, he replied, 'Ma, I will marry blindfolded the person you bring for me.' How many sons will say this? Even Orni and Shorna are rebellious and wilful despite the years my poor sister laboured to raise them. Such a devoted, respectful son will do the right thing by marriage as well," Aunty Reeha concluded.

The rice bowl was passed around the table. *Hilsa* fish curry had been cooked for Aunty Reeha. The fragrance of the freshwater fish quickly filled the room. It called forth the eaters' appetite, reminded them of childhood days when they fought siblings for the pleasure of the scarce fish eggs, and urged them to second and third helpings until their stomachs ached, bloated from overeating. Instead they waited. They deferred to Aunty Reeha offering her the first choice and insisting on piling exorbitant spoonfuls onto her plate. Eventually Baba was the one to be given the first pieces of the fish. For Orni who had to forgo lunch to lessen her protruding tummy, the thought of breaking the soft meat, sifting through the needle-thin bones, and increasing its heavenliness with the freshly steamed basmati rice, the long wait was a mouth-watering experience.

When it was her turn, Orni knew Ma's hawk eyes were watching, sizing the contents of her place. Orni enjoyed making Ma wait as she paused thoughtfully between spoonfuls of rice. Ma snatched her plate away just as Orni began to break down the clumps of rice.

"You must return to your diet. It's lucky they didn't examine you up close. You must shed the excess weight. You won't look good in a wedding sari," Ma said.

Aunty Reeha laughed. Orni resented Ma's unrelenting fault-finding. It angered her to be compared to Shorna and found lacking each time. Ma pushed half the rice onto another plate.

"This won't make me lose weight, but it will keep me awake."

"You can have as much water as you like," Ma said.

"Water's all I've had since breakfast."

Baba quietly asked Ma to let Orni eat in peace. It did not surprise Orni when Ma ignored his request, giving him more Hilsa instead. Orni knew her rice was destined to wait in the refrigerator acquiring age like she did until she sat for her next meal. Having touched it, the rice claimed Orni. It would come looking for her, bound as it was to her, culturally, physically, spiritually, psychically, perpetually. Her leftovers, her *jootha*, reminded her of her difference. It separated her from everyone, made her a spectacle to wonder at, filled her with apprehension. She wanted to devour it until she could feel nothing.

Ma had tried roti, bread and pasta in turns, trying to wrench Orni from the grains that easily took on the flavour of anything it was combined with. The others were adulterations – they were chunky and their individual tastes too distinct. Orni wanted only to eat until she could barely drag herself to bed to rest so she could recover from the stupor of fulfilment. She wanted all other thoughts to be squashed under the pain in her tummy as she struggled between regurgitation and ingestion. She wanted to focus. This alone was reason to marry, to leave. She would marry if only for the satisfaction of eating again.

The telephone rang in her parents' bedroom. Eating paused as Baba hastily shook the rice clinging to his fingers and hurried to answer it.

"It must be them," Aunty Reeha whispered.

"God willing," Ma whispered back, her eyebrows twitching.

Both sisters tiptoed towards the entrance of the bedroom, but refrained from crowding around Baba. They scanned Baba's immobile face. The hilsa was forgotten. Orni was forgotten. Even their darling Shorna did not matter. The message was more important; the caller would save them from disgrace.

Meanwhile Orni helped herself to fresh rice and more fish. She was not terrified of what they could say. Their agreement would be a temporary cause for jubilation followed by frantic pleas for loans to the extended family. Refusal was a dead-end. It hurt Shorna's chances. It lowered Orni's own expectations from life.

Baba and Ma's heads hung a little lower with each rejection. Tonight Orni would sleep peacefully cradled in herself without that churning sound in her stomach. Orni smiled to herself as she imagined the longed for contentment and oblivion as she drank water to assist each fistful.

"Thanks for letting us know," they heard Baba say as he hung up. Everyone re-entered the room as Orni sat before an empty plate.

"They said Shovon is thinking of doing his MBA abroad," Baba sighed.

His shrunken face acquired the haggard immobility of a mask. He stared towards Orni but did not seem to see her. There was no joy in saving Orni from the doom Shovon's family promised.

"Why would a forty-year-old man quit his well-paid job to do another Masters degree?" Aunty Reeha said.

A cry escaped Ma's lips as she dropped to the floor clutching her chest and moaned again and again, "Oh my ill-fated child!"

Orni watched Ma as Aunty Reeha comforted her. It was not the first time they were helpless or had failed as a family. Orni watched as Baba stood motionless. His inability to react reminded Orni of herself at the mall when she grappled with resignation, hope, hate and discontentment. The perpetual sadness caused by her besmirched all the family's joys. Shorna's engagement was tempered by the agonising fear it would be broken off once questions about Orni were eventually raised. The sister of an unwanted woman was equally unwanted. Yet Orni seemed to be forgotten for the tantalising moment. Shorna's future in-laws did not seem to care enough to inquire about a future relative, and this omission was equally questionable. When would they remember to ask? Would they reject Shorna when they discovered her elder, spinster sister?

Predestination, the reward of patience and endeavour, the dignity of human life, the right to decline, the promise of the next time – Orni explored the proverbial condolences while the rice in her mouth prevented her from speaking.

"My ill-fated child!" Ma began to beat her chest.

As the last of the rice was dislodged from the crevices in her mouth, a question began to form in Orni's mind. "Who?" Orni wanted to know. "Who are you referring to? Me or Shorna?"

About The Author

Fatema Johera Ahmed joined her spouse in Melbourne in 2013. While she hails from Bangladesh, Fatema views herself as a third culture kid, having spent her formative years in Myanmar, Kuwait and India. She seeks to resourcefully divide her ample time between housewifery, gardening, reading books of worth, writing, attending literary events and falling in love with her new home city.

MY STORY

BOL

My name is Bol. I am a Dinka man. This is my story. What I tell you is true; it is my truth. My story is not straightforward but complicated. My memory of events and time, well, it weaves in and out. And before I begin I must tell you certain things so you can understand who I am, what it means to be Dinka and about the war in my country South Sudan.

The Dinka are cattle herding people who occupy an arc of territory fanning out south and east from the border between Northern and Southern Sudan. Dinka country fringes the White Nile and the Sudd, the world's largest swamp. There are scores of Dinka counties of which the Tonj is where I live. It is 1989 and the Sudanese People's Liberation Army (SPLA) is the government's main opponent in Southern Sudan. There has been fighting for six years. The SPLA is fighting for control of our Dinka region. Clan tensions have escalated. Every chief in Southern Sudan is obliged to offer a number of boys in proportion to the number of villages and people he is responsible for. The seven chiefs in the Tonj County must hand over 500 boys to the war effort. When civil war first broke out, many boys and men volunteered. Twenty boys from our village volunteered because they want guns and to fight. None ever returned and what happened to them is a continuing mystery.

I am eleven. I don't measure time: not the days of the week, the months or dates. I remember what happens from the rhythms of the seasons, by how much water is around and if my country is green or the rains are late and the ground is dried out. We are Dinka. We are pastoralists. We treasure cattle and have herds of goat and sheep.

During the wet season, lasting from about April to November, we live in roomy conical huts with mud brick walls and thatched grass roofs. We grow crops of durra (sorghum, or millet, our staple grain) corn, peanuts, beans and pumpkins around our family compound. Beyond the crops and in the woodlands our cattle graze during the day.

In the dry season, we move to temporary camps closer to permanent water and greener pastures and live off stored grain and vegetables.

I am eleven and wear no clothes. It is the Dinka way, children do not wear clothes. It is not necessary and too hot. We have always done this. I am eleven and too young to be initiated. In Dinka culture groups of boys from about 12 to 15 undergo scarification on their faces to mark their coming of age.

My father died when I was four. We, my four brothers and two sisters, live with my mother and her people in her village Agurpiny. This is unusual in Dinka culture but my father was an orphan and my mother's people welcomed him when they married.

I live in our household compound. There is time for rest and for play. Despite our scattered compounds, Dinka are very close. Every evening in the village 'square,' we gather to tell stories and play games. Our animals are all around us.

I am in the fields weeding and see SPLA soldiers carrying guns coming down the path with the village leader Nyang-Akoc from my dead father's compound. I am afraid. I know they want mun: a tax our village must pay to fund the war for South Sudan's independence. Sometimes it is a cow or bull or kilos of sorghum. These soldiers are Dinka and must be treated as our guests. My oldest brother Akuei kills one of our goats and it is roasted over a fire. The adults discuss village news, the soldiers discuss how the war is going.

After our guests eat, the soldier in charge addresses Akuei formally, because he is the head of our household, not our mother. The soldiers say they have spoken to our father's brothers. My uncles have agreed we must contribute to the war effort.

We must contribute one son. Akuei volunteers. The soldiers stare at Akuei and say no. Akuei's index finger (his rifle finger) is broken. The soldier says 'You cannot fight with that finger'. My mother agrees, adding: 'You are the head of the household Akuei. You must stay and care for us'. Akuei accepts her judgement.

My second oldest brother Achuil cannot go either. He has survived a lightning strike. Surviving lightning gives him God's power, he is forever prohibited from using these powers or from firing a gun. And he is still going through ceremonies to heal the emotional effects of the lightning strike.

My next two brothers are twins. Twins are special and cannot be separated. The soldiers only need one boy; it is not possible to send just one.

I am Dinka. I know my duty. It is my duty to offer. I take mum aside and say I will go. I see my mother's heart drop. 'You can't go Bol. You are still small.' Akuei agrees.

'You are too young.'

My mother's brother and my father's brother disagree, 'It would be good. If Bol wants to go, he should go'.

Distressed, fearing my death, my mother pleads: 'He is not old enough to fight. No. Bol must stay'.

My uncle says 'Bol will have the chance to go to school. Life will be better for him'.

The soldiers argue among themselves if I should go. Finally one says, 'These are the kids for tomorrow. If we take him, he's not going to fight. He will go to school'.

Akuei, as family head, gives in, 'Bol is a good choice. He's a good runner and he's clever. Because of his speed and quick wit, he should find it easy to escape if he has to. It would be good if he has the chance to go to school'. My mother is in tears, but she has no choice and agrees.

When I leave the next morning I am neutral, not panicked or excited, just neutral. At eleven I think I could be somebody and it might be fun. I have no conception of war, I am a Dinka child and know only my compound, my family, my cattle and my clan.

My cousins Kuot and Kok have also been conscripted, so they

walk with me and the SPLA soldiers to Pankot. Kok and I are naked. Our first stop is the open-air market where clothes are sold. The soldiers buy me a brown *jellabiya*, the long gown usually worn by Arabs. I love my *jellabiya*, even though it drags on the ground because the market only sells clothes for adults. We march off to our army quarters located on the outskirts of Pankot.

In Pankot we are taught how to march, stand to attention and salute anyone above the rank of military trainee. Our trainers are harsh. I am not used to such treatment. The trainers tell us we must be tough to face battle, hardship and famine. I miss my home and family.

After three days of terrible training we are ordered to march on foot for Ethiopia. This is a three month dangerous journey. There are natural dangers—like being eaten by lions or crocodiles or drowning in rivers—and then there is starvation, dying from sickness and contaminated drinking water, or death from exhaustion and the hot sun. I know some of this and am afraid.

Our route goes through Nuer territory. The Dinka have long had tribal conflicts with them because the Nuer are cattle people too and there are fights over cattle and raids. There is also a Nuer remnant of the rebel group, the Anyanya. The Anyanya fought against the Sudanese Government during the first civil war, which ended in 1972 with a peace agreement. The Anyanya rejected the agreement and remained in the bush. When the 1983 civil war broke out, the Anyanya believed they should be the legitimate rebel group and not the SPLA. When SPLA recruits pass through Anyanya territory many are captured and are given the choice to fight with the Nuer or be killed.

A few days later on the road to Ethiopia I am walking with my two cousins in a chattering crowd of 1,800 men and boys. I hear my name being called. Mum! I see my mum. She has been camping on the side of the road waiting for me. My cousins and I sneak away and hide in the grass until everyone has left. We go home but the village is upset. They fear the SPLA will seek retribution because we deserted and return and take their cows. We must go back. My mum has no say in the matter, we must return.

This time, back on the road to Ethiopia with the SPLA, I escape on my own by telling the army men I must go to the toilet in the bushes. They don't wait for me. I run and run and get terribly lost, I have no idea where I am or in which direction is home. If I retrace my steps the army might find me. When night comes I cry and cry, frightened, and worried that a lion will eat me. Two days later I come to a village. They feed me and offer me a place to sleep and tell me how to find my village, which is actually very near. I find my mother's house. She hides me in her house overnight and the next day we go to my married sister's village, Ajak, far away, to keep me safe. Later my mum tells me the SPLA came, demanding to know where I am. She cries and moans and shakes her head. They take three cows in payment for my desertion.

In Ajak I am welcomed. I am an extra pair of hands and look after the sheep and goats. This is good because sheep and goats are kept closer to the village than crops and cattle and so I am in less danger of being found. After about five months, I return to mum's village because I feel the SPLA has forgotten about me and I am relatively safe.

The SPLA training camps in Ethiopia are closed after the overthrowing of the Mengistu Government. Boys are now being trained in the local district of Abii near Mayom-Abun, not that far away from my village. I decide to return to the army. I am still afraid that the SPLA finds me. After three escapes I could be shot. In Mayom-Abun we build a new training field, make our own huts, and dig latrines. We boys are the *Jess-Amer*, the child soldiers. In the *Jess-Amer* I am promoted to a 4-star sergeant major. At the age of about twelve, I am in command of a regiment—three platoons, more than 100 boys, some younger and some older than me. My regiment has boys from many different tribes, Nubians, Luo, Equatorians and Dinka.

To be a sergeant major is a big promotion. It happened after induction training. The leaders decide I am a smart boy. They test my physical strength. I must do many push-ups and stand in the hot sun for hours at attention. Some of the older boys don't like me telling them what to do and want to fight. I give them punishments like beatings, even sometimes to adult soldiers. It deters further challenges and they obey me. I do not beat boys myself. No, I have eleven boys to help me in my work. They are my *Basila Riaza*, an Arabic term for those who work for the sergeant major. We are quartered separately in our own hut.

The army is not too bad. There is a hierarchy. We wear camouflage like the adult army. I do military training, grass cutting and pole cutting for roofing but no cooking. As sergeant major cooking is not one of my duties. I like being in charge and do my job well, always focussing on order and what has to be done. In military training we learn how to march, to use guns and the tactics of guerrilla warfare.

We also have orders to compose songs. My regiment, but not me, make up patriotic songs about guerrilla warfare, the Arab domination of Sudan, stolen land and resources and how strong we are and how we have never being defeated—we *Jess-Amer* have yet to be in battles. On orders we sing these songs at night, during military parades and during exercises. These songs educate people about the war.

Army training camp life is hard and sometimes cruel. At night bushfly maggots come out of the ground, burrow into our skin and bite the way a tick does, causing a terrible itch, sores and wounds. To escape them, I build a bed using poles suspended off the ground on stick forks, and grass padding to try to protect myself. There is no privacy. You go to the toilet in an open trench running down next to the training field. We are only allowed to use the latrines during the permitted ten minute breaks. Boys with diarrhoea soil themselves; many boys die.

I am glad after a few months of training when our entire camp of 1,800 moves to Muddiria near the city of Juba in Equatoria Province. The South Sudanese capital, Juba, has fallen into the hands of Sudanese Government forces. In Muddiria, the adults are issued with guns and fight to recapture Juba. The fighting is intense. We boys continue with our daily chores, with our morning runs, military parades, exercises and singing in the evening. The whole regiment lines up, each platoon side by side, three rows deep of about 90 to 100 boys. We sing standing up for the first hour then we are allowed to sit.

I do not go to the frontlines until much later. I am part of the fighting force trying to protect a founder of the SPLA, Kerubino Kuanyin Bol, who switched back to the SPLA after defecting to the Government for four years. Now I am in Wau and for three months live and fight in trenches. My body is dry and my skin comes off because we don't have bedding or anything to sleep on, only bare ground. Government planes bomb and shell Wau every day. Smoke is how the bombers find us. I am very scared thinking about what could happen when I go to war, but when the action starts my fear vanishes. Fighting occupies my whole mind and body and I live only in the moment. My best friend Malong is killed at Wau, along with many boys from my clan. I fight in many different places.

Life changes. I am in my teens and attending school for the first time in Rumbek district in the Bahr El Ghazal Province. Our teachers are our former SPLA trainers. There are a lot of boys, boys from all over Southern Sudan. We are in a very small place to the northeast of Rumbek, in a town called Tiitkongkau.

None of us could read or write so we are all starting from scratch, learning our ABCs—the Roman alphabet. Dinka uses the same alphabet as English but with a few different vowels. In addition to technical military training we study English, Arabic, Dinka, maths, science and 'GHC'—geography, history and civics. Most of our schooling is in English because English is the SPLA language for official communications. Learning maths is not too bad, because most of it is formula so we could understand it with our basic English. For everything else it is very difficult; we know war, not classrooms and learning. If there is a Dinka teacher then sometimes we ask him for explanations during the break. There are no exercise books to write in. We learn to write in the dirt to remember what we are taught.

Today many of the child soldiers and other young people who were with the SPLA are in key positions in the Government. I think about two thirds of those who work for the South Sudanese

Government are former child soldiers. A number went off to America and to Cuba to finish their studies. The current Secretary General of the SPLA and the current Sudanese Foreign Minister, who is from Southern Sudan, were both educated in Cuba.

After a few months in Tiitkongkau attending school, Anthony Bol Madut, who is from my area and one of the SPLA commanders, came and took all the Tonj boys back to Tonj District to enrol us in school in Ananatak, near Mayom-Abun. There are just two teachers, Cirilo Chol Deng Akok and Achail Mangong Adoor, for 700 boys. They teach English, Arabic and maths. I am in grade three.

There is no school building; instead we sit outside on the ground under the mango trees and our teachers use a big whiteboard and write with charcoal, but unlike at Tiitkongkau here we use pencils and there is one exercise book for every two boys. We take dictation: the teacher writes something on the board and we read and memorise it, then we turn our backs to the board and recite from memory. I still remember learning the alphabet this way: A is for apple, B is for bat, C is for cat, D is for dog, E is for elephant and so on.

As well as classes and military instruction we still must make our early morning runs, have military parades, build our own houses, cook and clean. I do not cook because of my army rank. At Ananatak I am made an acting five stripe sergeant in charge of everybody. It is my job to keep order for the teachers and to ensure boys turn up for class.

After less than a year in Ananatak the fighting worsens. The SPLA cannot afford to feed and support us. I am sent to join the SPLA on the outskirts of Wau town in Warrap State where I am assigned as bodyguard and general factotum to an army doctor, a first lieutenant in the medical corps. He is still with the SPLA and is a colonel now.

As part of the medical corps I give out pills and other medicines under supervision, but I am really a servant. For the first time since I joined the SPLA I must cook. It is demeaning for a Dinka man from a good, well-off family, owning many cattle, to work as another man's servant, fetching, carrying, doing his cooking; it is, well, wifely work. Also I had gone from being a sergeant major in the *Jess-Amer* commanding many soldiers, to being at one man's beck and call.

If you are not an officer in the army, if you are an ordinary soldier, you are treated as nothing. They forget you are a human being. Even in the middle of the night if he wants something, no matter how trivial, he wakes me up and I must do it. I must wait until he finishes eating before I eat, and while I have my own rations they are meagre and he expects me to eat his leftovers. I never do, even though I am often hungry. It is the system; he is not a bad man.

One night he orders me to fetch water for one of his girlfriends. I refuse. 'You're not allowed to talk to your commander like that', he says.

Angry, I reply, 'It's not my job to get water for people who aren't soldiers'. I spend the night in gaol. The gaol is a small, fenced enclosure made of thorns, sharp and prickly so you can't escape.

Much later I am put in gaol for a second time. The commander of a platoon arrives from Warrap where there has been heavy fighting. They want to take me, minus my gun. 'I'm not going' I say. 'I don't want to be a soldier anymore. If you want to shoot me, then shoot me.'

I collect my belongings while they watch and I walk away. They don't shoot and they don't stop me.

'*Jess Amer*,' they say and shrug. *Jess Amer* also means someone who is very young and they know that your mind is perhaps not well formed, that you are young. So they let me go.

I go to the house of my eldest sister, Amel, who lives near Pankot and still the soldiers don't come for me, so I go home to my village. I am regarded as a child because I am not initiated, unlike the other young men of the same age as me. They are the real men and adults, not me who fought for them. They are warriors: guardians of the cattle camp against predators such as lions and hyenas and against enemy raiders. I am not scarified on the forehead in a pattern unique to my Dinka tribe. The SPLA does not allow initiations because it takes up to a month for the scar to form on the forehead after the cutting; recovery time interferes with the war effort. Wanting to be accepted by my village and my community and despite being already 18-years-old I decide to be initiated, only there is no ceremony for a long time. I go alone to the 'marker' man who conducts the initiations. He lives four hours' walk away in my older sister's village. Initially he is suspicious. It is against the law to scarify a soldier and he could go to gaol. I tell him I have been away at school so missed the ceremony. Finally he agrees and cuts my forehead. The cutting is very painful but I must show courage; it is my initiation, I am Dinka.

Now it is not so necessary to be initiated, and in fact the government discourages it. There are many men—Dinka and Nuer—in the army who have become government officials, or boys who live in towns and go to school who are not initiated and it does not go against them.

Back in my village I am accepted as a man with other boys of my age. We chase girls in our village and other nearby villages. Our boys' night drumming sessions are the best—like a local nightclub perhaps, but of course different. I do a bit of minding of the sheep and goats but mostly just enjoy myself.

After a period of some peace the civil war escalates again. The call goes out to all soldiers who returned home to report back for duty or be shot without any investigation. The SPLA would also punish my family and take more cows if I didn't go. I walk back to Mayom Abun, joining the crowds of soldiers reporting for duty. I am appointed to head up a platoon as my rank is still sergeant. We are sent to a place called Pagol, in Payam in Tonj district, to build bridges across marshland to enable convoys of troops and supplies to pass through the area. After perhaps three months my platoon must go to the local villages in the Tonj district to collect taxes, mainly in the form of cattle but also sheep. We visit a chief and, together, agree on the number of beasts to be supplied by each villager. The fighting is fierce now. The SPLA quickly captures the towns and cities of Yirol, Rumbek, Warrap and Tonj.

Wau fills up with people displaced by the fighting. Government forces hold Wau and prevent men leaving town. Many are afraid they will be killed on the road if they venture home. Crops aren't planted in many areas during the planting season. In 1998 there is famine in Bahr El Ghazal.

1998 is a terrible year. Hundreds of thousands of Dinka suffer severe malnutrition and many die of starvation. The constant raids by militias drive thousands from their homes in towns, while the looting of aid and the SPLA's recurring taxation of civilians weakens the peoples' capacity to cope with severe drought. My mother's two brothers (my uncles), two stepbrothers and a cousin die during the famine. The head of my family, my oldest brother Akuei dies sometime during the war. I am not sure when. All these deaths. It is heart breaking.

It is so hard to see people starving, especially children with their distended stomachs. They die; there is nothing you can do about it. I put my gun and my uniform aside to work as a civilian. Because I speak English I assist the UN to distribute food with aid drops, together with a regiment sized group of other boy soldiers.

I don't want to fight any more; I want to go to school. Whenever an army troop passes, I am taken from school and forced to serve. Schools are the most convenient places to capture young boys for the *Jess-Amer*. My life is very unstable. I have no control.

I hate being a soldier: there is no future, death faces you all the time and life is always uncomfortable. If you are an ordinary soldier you are treated as nothing. We boy soldiers are not paid. Being an officer is better; they live well—good accommodation, clothes and food—and you might be able to do something good. All around me I see boys who left to get an education returning as officers. I want an education.

In my civilian work I hear about Kakuma Refugee Camp in Kenya. The Sudanese Relief and Rehabilitation Association is based in Kenya and many Southern Sudanese work there. They return by airplane to Kakuma to see relatives. They are well dressed and educated and so I think this Kakuma must be a good place: a big city where everything that I need would be available and I would become educated, then I could return to my country, reunite my family destroyed by war and famine, rejoin the SPLA and fight for the self-determination of South Sudan.

Elijah Deng Majok is the head of the Sudanese Relief and Rehabilitation Association working with the UN in Thiet. An educated man, Elijah Deng believes in education and sees the waste of our young lives. He agrees to smuggle four of my cousins and me out of the country under an assumed identity. On 26 June 1999 I fly out from the Thiet airstrip under an assumed name to avoid detection by airport security men.

From Thiet we fly to Lokichogio, or Loki as we call it, a town just inside Kenya near the border with Sudan, a two-hour flight. Walking it takes three months. Kakuma is about 95 kilometres south of Loki, a two-hour drive away. It is a scary drive. We have a police escort because our convoy could be attacked and robbed by the local people, the Turkana.

The Turkana are true nomads: no permanent houses. Their land is very dry and they do not have a very good life. They see the refugee camp at Kakuma and what they see is people with more clothes, more food and with better access to water. Some of their women think they will have an easier life with a husband from the town or the camp and get pregnant; then their people get angry. Further, Kakuma is a very large camp taking up ten miles of Turkana territory. They do not like that either, so they come looking for food and clothes; sometimes they rob people to get what they need.

We reach Kakuma but must wait for two weeks outside the camp, sleeping on the hard floor of the veranda outside the reception area until we are registered for ration cards and allocated to a section of the camp. There are about 65,000 refugees living in the camp. We live next to other Sudanese, to Ethiopians, Eritreans, Burundians, Rwandans, Somalis; we share the same water point, queue at the same ration centre and go to the same school.

We are five people, my four cousins and I, squashed into one hut. It is a bit like the ones back home: conical with mud brick walls and a roof made of the local palm, *makuti*. We sleep on a large plastic mat on the floor. As soon as we are housed we rush off to register for school. Straightaway I go into grade three, quickly pass through grade four and jump to grade five. My classes are very large: 200 to 300 students in one class. This time each of us has our own exercise books to write in and textbooks. I love going to school. I am always in the top ten, sometimes sixth and occasionally number one. There is a lot of competition. If you are not in the top ten you are not regarded as knowing anything: you are not considered clever. If you are in the top ten people respect you.

We go to school five days a week. In primary up to grade seven we do twelve subjects, after that it is reduced to six. Our subjects include English, maths, science, health science, music, business, art and craft, geography, history and civics, and Christian religious education. I am a Catholic; my home village is Catholic. At Kakuma I am an altar boy on Sundays.

Even though I am grateful to be in Kakuma, life is very hard. The camp is crowded. Often we get up at 2.00 am to queue for food. Hungry, we stand all day in the hot sun, although we do have water to drink until we get food at 5:00 pm. We must build our own small house by making lots of mud bricks, and we sell some to buy iron sheets and poles for roofing the house. Making the bricks is one of the hardest jobs to do. It is physically demanding. My body is frail from famine and later, typhoid, and I still suffer from anaemia. We scrounge for clothes and shoes and sleep on the floor without bedding. It is hot all the time. There is never enough food and the drinking water is very poor. I am often afraid of being killed. From time to time Turkana attack the camp and kill many camp residents. When new, stronger fences are built we still do not venture outside the camp at night. There is no communication with my family.

My memories of Kakuma are full of sadness, yet I am glad I was educated and finished grade eight there.

I apply for resettlement in the West. At first it is to go to the United States because I have a cousin there who agrees to sponsor me. After 9/11, that door closes. My cousin, Aduot, has a Sudanese friend living in Australia. He agrees to sponsor me for a humanitarian visa in 2002 as a 'refugee minor,' a young refugee settling in Australia without parents or any other family.

In 2003 I arrive in Australia and am sent for settlement to Toowoomba in Queensland. I enrol in Year 9 at St Mary's College. It is so hard. I am the oldest in the class, very much older, the only black. They find my Kenyan English accent impossible while I cannot understand their Aussie dialect or accent. Many boys are rude; they jeer when I ask questions. Some of the teachers too are impatient. Life is so different.

But there are good people too. A friend, Matthew Booth, helps me to learn Aussie culture and language. A teacher, Miss Egan, is tough but expects me to do assignments on time and demands high standards. I work hard. By the end of Year 10 I am getting good marks. Then in Year 11 there are family troubles back in Sudan. One of my twin brothers dies in Sudan and the other twin is ill in hospital in Kenya. I need to send money to pay for his hospital bills, but I have only Centrelink payments and can't.

I am sad and find it difficult to concentrate on my studies. I drop out of school to work at a seedling nursery farm and study at night. I start a Certificate III in Accounting at TAFE in Toowoomba. I find a better job with more money in Brisbane in October and return to school at Southbank TAFE, finishing high school by doing Years 11 and 12 in the same year. English literature at Year 12 level is very hard for me: Shakespeare is a struggle; writing about it in the English language and understanding its subtleties is confusing. Much to my surprise I pass, although not well enough to go on to university.

Many students from my country, from other African countries and other overseas students find the Australian school system bewildering. Technology is also a barrier. The world of computers and the internet are like foreign countries to me and others like me. How can we perform the same as local students? Many of us do drop out.

At the end of 2006 during the summer vacation period, I visit Melbourne for a holiday. There are lots of Sudanese people here and I meet people I know from Kakuma. Melbourne appeals to me, so I move south. Since then I have continued with studying during the day and work in the evening. I can support myself and also send money back to my family in Sudan through my paid jobs—labouring and factory packing jobs—during the day and at night. I complete an Advanced Diploma of International Business and a Bachelor's in the same field. I am now enrolled in a Masters of Business at RMIT University.

I did work all the time for my community in the evening and on the weekends as a Dinka and Arabic interpreter with the police, in hospitals and local councils. Later I was elected youth leader for the Sudanese Community Association of Australia, taught some English and worked on a Dinka radio program. But now with the study required for the MBA and establishing my own business, a Registered Training Organisation—which is a place to train for the getting of certificates, diplomas and short courses—I have less time. I am still very close to the South Sudanese community. There is my family too. I am married with children. Life is busy.

Despite the difficulties of adjusting to life in a new country I am happy to have settled in Australia. Living here has restored my hopes, rebuilt my confidence and made me a stronger person. I am proud to be an Australian citizen, a citizen of a country that cares about its people. I am Dinka; I am Australian. My life is still full of challenges.

About The Author
Bol's life has been full of tumult since he was eleven; and yet he is full of resilience and hope for the future. In Australia he has created a home for himself, his wife and his children and is making his way.

HOW I LOST MY EYE

SIDO NDAYI

I had to leave my home because of ethnic violence. So I left my country the Congo, and lost everything I had. Now I was a refugee, a refugee from Africa in Africa. I had to start a new life. I have made a life of starting new lives.

In Zambia, I had been in the bush to forage for sweet potatoes. But the day I brought them to market there was a glut and my crop was left to rot.

I was almost broke. With what little money I had left I bought some cooking utensils, pulled in some favours and started a small restaurant. Now when I say restaurant, it was really a straw hut. At night I sewed. During the day, I cooked.

Tension was building in my arteries from all the pressure and stress. I went to hospital.

'You have a serious problem,' said the doctor. 'Your retina is detached because of arterial pressure'.

I felt it was from my stress; the stress of surviving. I was told there was no one that could treat me. I was discouraged.

All of a sudden it felt like my eye was moving around in my head. It didn't hurt, but it felt like my eye was turning inside my head. I was told treatment was only available in South Africa or in Tanzania.

In Tanzania I saw an Australian doctor. I remember listening to the buses. The UN buses in the street. A crow shat on my head. It was a lot of shit. I thought, *This a bad sign*. I thought *Any bird, just not a crow*. I thought I should take it as a sign not to have the operation. But since the UN had offered to pay for the procedure, I accepted.

The doctor said he operated on anyone. For anything. Can you imagine one person operating on twenty plus people a day? In Africa you wait in line for an operation. It's like an abattoir. Poverty is worse than death.

The operation lasted four hours. I remember waking up; the anaesthetic had worn off. Mosquitos were everywhere, even under the mosquito netting. I swatted at a mosquito and hit myself in the eye. I cried like a little girl.

The eye still hurts. The operation was not well done. I now understand that doctors specialise. That doctor did what he could.

It traumatised me though. I was afraid of everything after that: of taking the elevator; of driving; even of the stove, I was afraid it would burn me.

I started cleaning houses; transferring the physical pain into the intensity of my cleaning. But I had to learn to accept my new self.

I lost the eye, perhaps because I did not accept my suffering but threw myself into work, avoiding it. I was really unhappy when I think about it now. If I had had some money, even $300, I could have gone to South Africa and got myself treated properly. But I didn't. That hurts more than the pain from my eye. Poverty is worse than death.

It still hurts. But I have to accept it, because if you accept you win. Beating pain is not easy. But I won. When Moses led his people out of Egypt to the Promised Land they kept going, despite the difficulties they faced along the way. They didn't return. Neither will I.

About The Author

Sido was born in the Congo to middle class parents on a date she prefers not to disclose. The eruption of ethnic violence forced her to leave her home and flee to the south of the country. The situation worsened and she spent several years as a refugee in various African countries, including Zambia and Tanzania.

She was granted refugee status in Australia and arrived in the country in 2007. She lives in Melbourne where she founded Mama Destiny, an organisation that supports Congolese youths in crisis.

HAPPY KIDS HARBOUR

YING BAI

Exercise
The sun is rising in the sky,
The flowers are happy and twist their vines.

The birds tweet-tweet on a branch,
Early to bed and early to rise.

Shake, shake, shake your hands,
Stomp, stomp, stomp your feet.

Let's all exercise and follow this beat.
Nod, nod your head.

Turn, turn, turn your waist.
I am a good child, *healthy, wealthy and wise*.

Noodle song
I love noodles, how about you?

We walk to the noodle shop,
What do we do?

Say 'Hello, chef!' and order our food,
Take a seat and wait for our noodles.

Eyes, eyes, what do you see?
We see…'Noodles, noodles, noodles.'

Nose, nose, what do you smell?
I smell…'Noodles, noodles, noodles.'

Ears, ears, what do you hear?
We hear…'Noodles are coming!'

Mouth, mouth, how do they taste?
'Yum, yum, yum, noodles taste nice!'

I love noodles, so do you?
When we leave the noodle shop,
What do you do?
We pay and say 'Thanks, chef!

We love your noodles,
Have a lovely day!'

Finger animals
I have two little hands, with ten little fingers,
One finger here, one finger there,
I am now a cow 'moo moo moo'.

I have two little hands, with ten little fingers,
Two fingers here, two fingers there,
I am now a rabbit, 'hop hop hop'.

I have two little hands, with ten little fingers,
Three fingers here, three fingers there,
I am now a kangaroo, 'jump jump jump'.

I have two little hands, with ten little fingers,
Four fingers here, four fingers there,
I am now a puppy-dog, 'woof woof woof'.

I have two little hands, with ten little fingers,
Five fingers here, five fingers there,
I am now a reindeer, 'leap leap leap'.

About The Author

Ying Bai's rhymes and songs are for bilingual Mandarin Chinese-English playgroups for children aged five and younger. Ying's first language is Mandarin, but her Australian born daughter is growing up in an English speaking environment. Ying wrote these educational yet fun children's rhymes because her daughter was able to pick up words and sounds easily from both languages. The rhymes can be set to music and either Mandarin or English words can be used. It is Ying's way of preserving a link to their shared culture and heritage. Ying hopes that you will enjoy reading them as a tribute to her love for watching her child adapt to a country that is a new home for them both.

THE LOST GIRL

HEBA

My maternal grandmother was tough, always yelling and screaming. My maternal grandfather met my father when my father was hired to teach religious studies to children. He saved his money carefully. My grandfather admired this, and loved him. He suggested he should marry his daughter, my mum. I know they had a good marriage. My dad was a dark, tall man. He was a good provider and never came into the house with empty hands—he always had fruit or meat. When he got paid he was generous to everyone. He was welcoming and looked after people outside of the family—people still talk about him to this day. My mum was fair, and a quiet person who liked being at home. I don't remember a lot about her.

My family was always going back and forth between Somalia and Ethiopia in the Ogaden region. My dad had two houses, two wives and a big coffee farm in Ethiopia, which is still there. He was working at the Somali Embassy in Ethiopia. In the 1977 war the Ethiopian authorities targeted him because he was successful. They imprisoned him, beat him, and they put his feet in boiling oil.

My mum didn't know what to do because she didn't know anyone where we were living in Somalia, so she took us back to Ethiopia for a while to live with her parents, but then her parents died too. The Ethiopian government took the house, claiming it could do this because we were Somali. Dad escaped from jail and took my mum and us kids back to Somalia.

My mum was killed by gunfire when I was four-years-old. My dad died when I was six. At this point some of the older kids had grown up and moved away; the ones who had stayed together, including me, left Somalia and went to Djibouti.

One day when I was eight and out shopping for *eid* with my big sister, two police cars stopped us to check our IDs. We had no ID papers in Djibouti. One policeman took my big sister and the other took me and put us in separate cars. Ruqia later told me she insisted the driver of her police car stop, but the man spoke a different language and didn't understand her, or didn't want to.

There were other people in the car I was in, mostly men, but also another girl who wouldn't look at me. They drove us over the border and dumped us in Somalia. There were people everywhere. I cried and cried until I fell asleep under a tree. When I woke up it was night and a woman was standing over me. She was a businesswoman travelling from Djibouti to Somalia. She took me to her home and promised that I would be able to go home, but the next day she put me to work as her maid. She was an evil woman.

Her husband was nice. Their daughter was living away from home while she was studying but their son was there. He was ten years older than me.

I worked all day, wasn't allowed to leave the house and slept in the kitchen at night. It was hard work and I was very small. She would punish me when I made mistakes. One time, visitors came late at night and the evil woman woke me up and told me to make tea. I was still half asleep trying to make the tea and I burnt the sugar. She pulled my hair so hard that even today I still get headaches. After the horrible hair pulling I cut all my hair off so she couldn't do it again.

From when I was aged eight to age thirteen the son came for me every night. The first time, he came into my room at midnight and I screamed and he ran away. The father came in. I told him someone had come into the room. He told me to keep the door locked.

The next night the son broke the lock and attacked me. I screamed. Again the father arrived and I told him it was his son who attacked me. He questioned his son. The son said I was lying. The father told the evil woman what happened and she called me a liar and beat me badly with a stick and threatened to cut my throat. I was too scared to say anything ever again.

Later, I drank a bottle of liquid we used to kill mosquitos, hoping it would poison me. The father found me; my mouth was foaming. He took me to the hospital. The evil woman didn't speak to him for ten days after that.

I was jealous when I heard someone died.

I got pregnant when I was 13. The evil woman only noticed when I was eight months along. I told her it was her son who was the baby's father. She beat me again, but her husband intervened. She said she would deny the baby a surname until DNA testing was done.

I gave birth to my daughter in the kitchen. A woman took my daughter away while I had to stay in the kitchen. I was only allowed to see my baby to breastfeed her and two days after the birth I had to work again although I was in terrible pain. Straight after I gave birth the son's attacks continued. I remember there was blood everywhere, a trail of blood.

When the DNA test proved who the father was the evil woman forced me to marry her son. A man came to the house to conduct the engagement. I wasn't allowed to come out of the kitchen. The evil woman said I was young and scared to talk but happy to be getting married. He didn't even see me.

I made friends with another lady who was brought in to help around the house, but when the evil woman found out we were friends she expelled her. Another older lady started working there and she was friendly to me too.

I told a friend of the family's daughter, who was living next door, what was happening to me, even though I was scared to trust her. She could help me—a man would come with a car in the next few days and take me to Ethiopia. I didn't know how I would escape with my baby but she came up with a plan.

She asked the evil woman to borrow me to help clean her house and asked for me to bring the baby too. The evil woman said she could borrow me but my daughter had to stay. I went to the friend's house and waited. After a while she told the evil woman she still needed my help for more cleaning but my baby needed to be fed. The evil woman agreed and handed over my daughter. Then my friend called her brother; the man who was going to come and take us away.

I was so scared, but I managed to escape with my daughter who was only three months old.

My neighbour's brother drove for 14 hours to Ethiopia. He wanted to take me to his family's home to eat and to rest, but I was scared and said no. He kept offering, telling me it wasn't safe to leave us on the street. Eventually I agreed.

His family was nice to me. His wife realised she knew of my father. I asked her if she knew anything about my siblings. She said she knew my big sister and my brother were living in Melbourne, Australia. She knew my big sister's brother-in-law who lived nearby. He came to talk to me and said he had never heard of me. He gave me a number to call my big sister. The wife took me to the phone box to call her.

When big sister answered the phone I said, 'It's me, your little sister'.

'She's dead,' said my big sister.

I told her everything that had happened since we last saw each other.

It was during this I realised I was pregnant again from the man I had been forced to marry. I had a second child, my son, at home. I couldn't go to the hospital because someone might pass on the news that I was there.

A few months later my big sister arrived from Australia to visit me in Ethiopia. She paid the rent for an apartment for me and my children while I was applying for us to come to Australia.

I got a call from the embassy telling me to go to Nairobi for an interview. I was so afraid to go as I had to leave the kids. Even though my neighbour offered I didn't trust anyone, so my brother-in-law looked after them.

When I crossed into Kenya the police requested a bribe. I got through and got to the interview where friends of my sister were able to help. An Australian lady interviewed me. She asked me how I felt about leaving my kids and I told her I was having nightmares that my son would fall down the stairs at my brother-in-law's house. I was always crying in those days.

The Australian lady said she would go and get my children from Ethiopia. She took a photo of me to show to the kids to reassure them that they should come with her.

She returned with my kids. When I met them at the airport she asked, 'How do you feel now?' I cried and cried and said thank you.

The day I got my visa was my beautiful day. I thought Australia was heaven.

I arrived in Melbourne in 2002, on a Wednesday. My big sister and her family met me at the airport and took me to the house where I was going to stay temporarily. I thought this was a beautiful country, full of money. Uncles and aunties had sent money to go shopping in Africa for the things I needed before I left, but I said, 'No, I want to buy things in Australia'.

My first year in Australia was very hard. My worst day was in my second week in Melbourne. My big sister drove me and the kids to childcare and school, but she took a shortcut and when I went to pick them up on foot in the afternoon I got lost. I couldn't speak English and I had no phone. Thankfully the school contacted my big sister and she picked my children up and took them to my house.

My big sister helped with many things, but she only helps people for big things, not small things. She is a very private, difficult person, but I love her.

When I first arrived she took control of my payments and I didn't have enough money for food or transport. She signed me up for a phone account but then she would use the phone to make international calls while I was at school. The bills were so big, I didn't know what to do. Overcome with worry I began vomiting blood and ended up in hospital. I felt so sad that my sister did this. I didn't think these things would happen in Australia. Finally I changed the bills into my name.

Today, I don't see my big sister but I would like to. My brother says I will end up forgetting her like she is dead.

In Melbourne I told a few people my story, but then I stopped. My community rejected me because my daughter was born out of wedlock, and men who were interested in a relationship with me backed away. Often other children would say hurtful things to my daughter, things she didn't understand. It was just easier to keep to ourselves. I have friends from many other countries but not many friends from my community.

In 2009 I visited all the places that my parents had been. People told me they would be witnesses for a case against the government about my father's confiscated property, but I haven't decided to do that yet. A lady also told me she knew the man who attacked me and he had apologised, as he knew he had done the wrong thing. But I don't care about that.

I got in contact with a cousin of mine in New Zealand. After we got to know each other we married. I visited him there but had to return to Australia without him because he didn't have a visa yet. Back in Australia I found out I was pregnant. Soon after that my husband and I divorced because he felt pressured by the community gossip about me.

When our son was two my ex-husband came from New Zealand to Australia to see him for the first time. He saw this family and what was here for him. He begged me for another chance at our marriage. We have been together now for several years. We had three more children together.

When my eldest daughter was fifteen and my son was thirteen I told them what had happened to me and who their father was. My daughter is curious to see him, but I said no. My son says he never wants to see him.

I worry a lot about my children. I rely on my daughter a lot to help me but she has had such a different life to mine. My son is very thoughtful and always looks after me. Still I worry: I had a dream that my son is going to jump into a well, the kind of well that we have back home.

Before, I always wondered why these terrible things happened to me like they did. Were they some kind of punishment from God? Now I don't ask why such bad things happened to me so much. Sometimes I see the things that happened to me like they are on TV. And I know God wouldn't punish an innocent child. Before a child is born, the Creator plans their every step.

About The Author

Heba is from Somalia and came to Australia in 2004. She is a mother to six children, aged from one to seventeen years. She lives in Melbourne with her family. Heba feels she has a lot of problems due to her terrible experiences. Writing her story was a way to help herself.

ANGUISH TO ACCEPTANCE

KALI PAXINOS

It was a Saturday night and Anna had bought a new frock to wear at the farewell dinner for her friend Maria. Yianni looked elegant in his dinner suit, white shirt and black bow tie. He usually started work at 6.30 pm, working as a drink waiter at a high-class restaurant.

They had been living in their home for over twenty years, raising their five children who had left to live their adult lives. It was a good home. By the front door there was a bookcase. There were novels, sheet music, journals from America and London, translated poetry from relatives living overseas. The telephone sat on the top shelf. The telephone was the link to their grandchildren. It sat proudly atop the bookcase and pulled at them like a magnet.

Yianni migrated to Australia when he was sixteen, glad to leave Greek life behind him—the poverty and the family tragedies. 'I had to get out so I could breathe', he would often tell Anna.

Anna was born in Australia. Her parents had migrated from Greece about 1915.

As Anna and Yianni stood before the large mirror in the bedroom, remembering the early years of their arranged marriage, Anna asked, 'Yianni, do you remember the Indian man who spoke to us in Mildura? The day we walked with an Indian worker around the grape vines? He said we would have ten children'.

'He was half right', Yianni replied, 'we've got five and they're all beautiful'.

They heard the rumbling of thunder. It increased their fear and anguish. Rain began falling and, within seconds, it became a waterfall. The windscreen wipers slowed and soon were useless. Then they stopped altogether. Chaos! Cars slowed but one red Holden car started weaving from lane to lane with increasing speed. Yianni was driving blind; the highway lights were now not functioning, horns blared. Anna shouted for him to move to the side of the road and stop.

'I can't see', he yelled back.

The squall eased; the rain stopped as suddenly as it had begun. They drove on.

As they entered the Bendigo police station Yianni turned to Anna and put his arm around her.

'Come Anna, we will walk together.'

At the end of the passage was an empty window. A police woman responded to the ringing bell.

'Please, I want to see my Sam', cried Anna. 'What has happened? Why is he here? I want to see him.' Yianni tried to calm her. Anna's agitation increased as the female constable attempted to give an explanation.

Although it was only minutes later it seemed like hours before Inspector Morris introduced himself. Anna dried her eyes. She noticed how very tall he was. His voice was soft and gentle. Anna sensed he was a good man. Inspector Morris guided them towards the large holding room where Sam was. They tried to suppress their anxiety. It was utter chaos. They couldn't see Sam.

A group of young men yelling obscenities were wrestling with three police officers, who pushed them to sit and cuffed their hands to the chairs.

The police-guards had guns strapped to their waists and their voices were loud and threatening. The tallest one clutched his gun as if he was about to discharge it. His blue eyes were hard and fierce.

The stench of alcohol filled the room. Two young girls, also handcuffed and no more than sixteen years old, sat next to the angry young men. One of the girls was sobbing, the other girl, with multi-coloured streaks through her blonde hair, was yelling and swearing at the policemen. All the yelling and the obscene language sent a shudder through Anna's spine.

Inspector Morris walked them to a small table near the window where it was quieter, and asked them to wait. He'd bring Sam to see them. Anna felt comfortable with the inspector. He didn't carry a gun. The inspector spoke very quietly; Anna had to listen hard. 'Before I get Sam, I'd like you to know that we haven't picked up Sam for the kind of behaviour you can see in this room. He seems to have other problems.'

Anna looked at Yianni. What does he mean Sam has other problems?

Yianni was worried, something serious has happened he thought.

Inspector Morris returned with his arm around Sam whose black cap was pulled low over his eyes. He looked different: unshaven, his hair matted, his jeans and shirt torn, his jumper back to front and only a battered pair of thongs on his filthy feet. He seemed to be in another world.

Anna jumped out of her chair and ran towards him. Yianni tried to stop her. Sam put his hands over his head and looking only at the floor. He said, 'Go away'.

Inspector Morris calmed Sam, explaining that he would help him sort out his problems but needed to speak with his parents first. Sam shook his head. 'I only want to sit next to you.' The inspector sat. Sam sat down next to him but refused to even glance at Anna and Yianni.

'Why won't you look at us Sam?' Anna cried.

Yianni placed his hand on the table towards Sam and quietly said, 'You didn't come home last Saturday for our music session. I missed you'. Gradually, Sam lifted his head to look at Yianni. In her heart Anna knew he wasn't really seeing them, he wasn't here in this awful place he was somewhere else, but where?

Inspector Morris gave them the statement Sam had given to the police. 'I'll leave you now to read it and then we'll speak in my office.' He left.

'Why did you take so long?' Sam yelled.

'What have you done Sam?'

Sam wrapped his arms around his chest and refused to talk.

'Please, Sam, tell us what has happened that has brought you to this police station.'

'I can't tell you because you won't believe me, it's my secret. The police wouldn't listen to me. They pushed me into the police van. I want a cigarette. I'm hungry. Please don't believe the police, I haven't done anything.' Sam kept repeating these words in an increasingly higher pitch. His voice chilled Anna. Where was her son?

A voice over the inter-com asked Mr and Mrs Petropolis and Sam to report to Inspector Morris.

Anna tried to hug Sam. He shrugged her off and looked at his father. 'Please Dad, can you get me a cigarette?'

'Yes mate, but after we speak to the policeman.'

Inspector Morris sat at his desk checking his computer; there was a cupboard in the corner, lots of folders and three hard back chairs like the ones in the holding room. There was no window. It resembled a police cell. He asked if they had read Sam's statement.

'It doesn't make sense', Yianni said.

'He writes scripts for plays', Anna tried to explain, 'the statement reads like a play'.

'Anna', said Yianni, 'this isn't a script. All Sam had to do was explain what happened.'

Anna nodded; tears ran down her face.

'Something is seriously wrong with Sam', explained the Inspector. 'He will be charged with entering a lady's home. She was not home at the time Sam came to her house. The door was open. When the lady came home she found him sleeping in her bed. Sam will be notified about the details of the court case: trespass and breaking and entering, whatever the charge is. In the meantime, I suggest you contact your doctor. Sam seems to be showing symptoms of mental instability.'

'Sam, you slept in a woman's bed?' shouted Anna. 'Who was she? How could you? Why? Sam, you're a good boy.' Inspector Morris was listening quietly.

Sam just stared at Anna as if she was a stranger. Yianni shook his head in disbelief as he reread the statement.

'I need a smoke, let's go home Dad, please Dad don't listen to him, he doesn't understand, he's only a cop.'

'Inspector Morris you are so wrong', Anna cried. 'My Sam is a good boy, he is not mental. How could you say my Sam is mental? He writes stories, he is a good actor.' Her voice was trembling. Nothing was wrong with Sam. He was her son, her good son.

As they left the interview room, Sam noticed a man at the counter smoking a cigarette.

He asked for a cigarette. 'No problems', the man replied. Sam's hand shook as he lit the cigarette.

'I know how he feels', the man said.

No you don't, Anna thought. I'm his mother and I don't.

Sam's car was in the car park and needed petrol and Yianni had the keys.

'Dad, I'm going to drive home in my car.'

'No Sam, Mum will come with you', Yianni explained, 'you know your mother doesn't drive and I won't allow you to drive alone. I know you are an excellent driver and I'm going to trust you to drive your car taking Mum with you.'

Grimly, Anna agreed.

'Sure Dad. Can we get a pack of cigs and a pie before driving home?'

Maybe Sam was all right, Anna thought. He'd recovered. Everything would be back to normal.

Sam was driving carefully and she could see Yianni in the rear vision mirror.

Sam started to laugh. 'Mum, I need to come back to Bendigo to collect twelve feathers from the swans along the river and twelve stones from the Bendigo Arts Centre. When I do this I will get instructions how to reach outer space.' Anna clutched her handbag, her breathing was shallow. Is he rehearsing a script?

He'd performed with a theatre company a few years ago and liked quoting sections from the plays of Shakespeare and had a fascination with reading the legends of the Greek Gods.

'Sam, be careful you're driving too fast, you have to turn left at the intersection.'

'Mum you have to understand. I must return to Bendigo, don't tell me what to do.' Traffic was heavy as they entered Melbourne's busy streets and Anna was scared. She glanced at Sam, could sense his anger, so she stopped talking.

'Mum you can't stop me going to Bendigo next Saturday', Sam screamed. Anna was exhausted. It was way past midnight. Cars were speeding past them. They're drunk, Anna thought. At least Sam wasn't drunk. The thought didn't bring her comfort. Maybe it would be better if he were drunk. Drunk she understood. She switched on the car radio and an Irish ballad filled the car. She looked in the rear vision mirror: no Yianni!

'Sam we've lost your father.'

'He knows the way', said Sam, and then they were home. Sam quickly got out of the car, unlocked the house door and headed for the kitchen. Anna found him at the table holding the remains of the leg of lamb and tearing the meat with his hands. Silently she watched Sam finish eating and then flop onto the couch, fully clothed and unwashed.

The clock ticked: 1 am and still no Yianni! Anna rang emergency but they couldn't help. She rang the local police. They promised to contact the central division and let her know if they had any information. She wanted to call her children, have her children around her. Why alarm them? Better to wait until the police rang; but she was frightened, couldn't sit still. She paced around the house like a wild animal.

5.30 am and still no Yianni. He was gone, never coming home. She couldn't think straight—ideas, thoughts flashed in a jumble. Sam didn't have a mental problem. He's normal, he's not mental she kept telling herself. Where was Yianni?

'Anna, Anna, open the door, I've lost my keys. I had to walk. I ran out of petrol. The phones were all vandalised.' Anna opened the door to an exhausted Yianni. His clothes were wet, his hair dishevelled and he had fear written all over his face. 'How is Sam?'

Yianni had walked for hours, lost in the dark and the rain. Only when he'd recognised the park where Sam and his brothers played footy did he know he was nearly home.

They went to bed. What a relief to be in her own bed with Yianni by her side. She didn't dream.

The next morning Anna rang the family doctor. He would be there before lunch time. Anna was anxious to wake Sam. Yianni was still snoring after his marathon walk.

It seemed impossible to wake Sam. What would Dr McKenzie think? He had delivered all her five children. A ring at the front door awoke Yianni but a call to Sam went unanswered, he lay on top of his bed still wearing his filthy clothes with his hat pushed over his eyebrows.

'Leave me alone, don't hassle me', he yelled.

Anna retreated to the living room. She was calm when Dr McKenzie arrived. Anna and Yianni explained the events at the police station and gave him Sam's statement. After reading it he suggested he try to speak to Sam alone in his bedroom.

Sam mumbled he didn't want to talk. Dr McKenzie persisted. Sam sat and looked at the doctor. I want to eat something first. He went into the kitchen and slurped down cornflakes as if it were his last meal. Anna loitered just beyond the kitchen door and saw how cautious Dr McKenzie was not to say anything that might agitate Sam.

'You know Doctor, I have grown four inches since you saw me when I had the flu', said Sam in a high pitched voice. 'Why are you here? Has Mum got a migraine headache? Can you explain to Mum how important it is for me to go to Bendigo? I must go and collect twelve feathers and twelve stones and then I will get instructions how to reach outer space.'

'Sam, why don't you go into the bathroom and have a shower, then I will talk to you and your mum and dad.' Sam walked quietly into the bathroom.

That's a good sign Anna decided as she sat at the kitchen table, anxious to hear what Dr McKenzie had to say.

'I think he is showing signs of psychosis. I'm concerned about him and he must be seen by a psychiatrist. He's changed so much since I saw him six months ago. I will give you a referral to attend the local mental health clinic. It is important that one of his parents go with him. I will speak to Sam and tell him he must go to the clinic because he has to explain his behaviour when he goes to court. Please ring me if you need any help'. Dr McKenzie's voice showed real compassion.

Psychosis, what kind of word was psychosis? What did it mean? Anna stared at Yianni and Yianni stared back. It made no sense. He was just as bewildered as she was. One minute Sam was strange, then he would be like the old Sam who played hockey on Saturday and football on Sunday. His bedroom was full of trophies. Now they tell us he has to see a psychiatrist? We are a good family.

'What has happened?' cried Anna.

Yianni was silent, his hands over his head. Then he started hitting his head. 'It's that curse again, just when things were working themselves out.'

Yianni and Anna had planned to sell their house and buy a cottage near the sea with a lot of land. Yianni loved to fish. He would grow vegetables, plant fig and olive trees and perhaps a grape vine. 'We must have four chickens', he would tell his friends. 'I'll ride my bike to the shops.' Anna loved the sea too. She had such happy memories of watching her young children learn to swim then run along the sand collecting sea shells. Now would be the time for her to sit under the sun umbrella and read. They'd build small units on the land so the family and grandchildren could come for holidays. They would have a goat. Yianni had beautiful memories of taking Sam, as a two year old toddler, to the market to buy a baby goat. The children called him Bippy. Sam's sister would feed Bippy warm milk from a coca-cola bottle with a discarded teat.

Anna saw the sea retreating, the cottage, the units. What did signs of psychosis mean? It meant clinics and psychiatrists.

Anna took Sam to the clinic. A young psychiatric nurse listened to Sam's bizarre story and read the police report. Anna kept interrupting and wanting to tell her version of the story.

'Sam has a vivid imagination and is interested in writing plays. He is very talented and wants to act.'

At the end of the interview the nurse explained she needed to talk to the senior psychiatrist.

Anna and Sam were left in the corridor. Sam paced and started laughing over nothing. 'I'm going to Bendigo on Friday and you can't stop me', Sam shouted in a high pitched voice as other people in the corridor stared.

The nurse reappeared with pills and said the psychiatrist would see him in a month. Anna was stunned. She had questions. She had worries. Pills and tablets? Where was the help Sam needed? One month! A lifetime!

Sam took the tablets and within three days a sad, forlorn Sam wearing his father's dressing gown shuffled up and down the corridor looking like an old man. Every few minutes he would laugh. Anna rang her children with the grim news.

It was difficult for Anna to explain what had happened to their brother. It took quite a while for them to absorb all the details. They listened, and with great sadness each one wanted Anna to know that they would always help her and accept the decisions that she and their father made. It's an illness, we have to understand he is our brother he is our mate. Anna knew her children would help their brother.

'He could have some kind of mental illness', her son Paul said. Anna immediately had a vision of Sam locked in a psychiatric hospital, crouched in a corner with unsympathetic nurses. She was determined never to allow anyone to admit him to any institution.

Anna blamed herself. She had or hadn't done something. That's why it was her fault. It was always the mother's fault. People told her that. When Yianni heard her say these things he tried to comfort her. 'That's nonsense Anna, please don't blame yourself, you have been such a good mother to all the children.'

The guilt lay heavy upon her.

At Sam's next appointment Anna again requested to speak to Dr Flynn and, thankfully, he agreed. Dr Flynn was a very tall man, early forties with a Scottish accent. His calm voice and gentle smile calmed Anna. Sam was continually laughing. Anna was so embarrassed she could hardly get out her words.

'Can I call you Anna?' said Dr Flynn.

'Of course', she smiled. Immediately she trusted this man.

Dr Flynn explained Sam had symptoms of a serious mental illness.

'He is so different now, doctor, he has changed, he's not the same Sam anymore. He pushes me away, he often won't talk to me and he is really rude. Why has he changed so much?' Anna's eyes filled with tears.

'These symptoms suggest that he may have the beginnings of schizophrenia.'

Anna gasped. It can't be. He is a good boy, why has he got this?

Dr Flynn had few answers. 'If he takes his medication his symptoms may gradually lessen.'

It was a small promise and it was not what Anna wanted to hear. She wanted her son back.

Sam disappeared into his bedroom, locked the door and talked to himself. The enormity of Sam's mental illness sat in the living room like an unwanted guest who refused to leave.

Yianni took the diagnosis of schizophrenia as another curse put on his family. 'Why?' he kept repeating. One thing Anna knew; Sam's illness, his strangeness, would not be kept a secret, despite the curse or maybe because of the curse.

Yianni explained to relatives and friends what had happened and insisted the whole family must support Sam. We have difficult times ahead, but first we must learn many things, and above all we must live our lives sensibly and continue with our work. And this is exactly what happened.

Anna learned by joining the Schizophrenia Fellowship. Yianni encouraged her. It was too much for Yianni. His education was a stumbling block despite his good spoken English. He wouldn't be comfortable there and Anna understood. It was her job to protect her son and her husband.

Schizophrenia, Anna came to realise, remained the unwanted guest—always demanding, always unexpected and sad making. There were days when Sam would sleep until five in the afternoon and then walk up and down the street, sometimes laughing, sometimes crying.

Anna attended training programs, read many articles and joined groups that supported families in understanding how to cope with this difficult illness. She learned techniques of meditation.

The court case finally came around. The magistrate was sympathetic, and after he read the report from the treating psychiatrist, Sam was discharged. However he had to attend the clinic regularly for treatment. The clinic was a constant in all their lives.

Yianni retired. It was his dream to return to the island of his birth for a holiday. They'd take Sam with them. It would be good for him. The legends and climate would be helpful for his recovery. Sam's psychiatrist was concerned but Sam wanted to go.

Anna boarded a Qantas flight to Greece with a bagful of Sam's medication. Sam packed three books relating to ancient Greek mythology. He slept for most of the first leg of the trip but when he awoke he was agitated and confused. Anna gave him his tablets.

Arriving at Singapore airport, Sam wanted to look at some books across from the coffee shop.

Reluctantly Anna agreed. He'd only be fifteen minutes. Sam didn't return. Anna panicked; Yianni panicked. The police advised them to board the plane, explaining that it wouldn't leave until all passengers returned. Ten minutes later Sam appeared, confused, shambling, not understanding, accompanied by a flight attendant who'd found him sitting slouched in a chair at the airport lounge.

Anna worried. Had they done the right thing bringing Sam?

In chaotic Athens Sam was quiet but seemed confused. The next day they boarded the ferry. During the trip Sam spent most of the time wandering around the boat smoking. Anna worried about what Sam was doing. Yianni chatted with other passengers some of whom he had known as a child. They had migrated to America or South Africa and, like him, were revisiting their homeland for a holiday. All were now old; some had walking sticks, others had hearing aids, many had false teeth.

The ferry turned and they could see the coastline of the island. Yianni called Sam to the deck and pointed ahead. 'This is the home of our people', he said. Anna watched, delighted. Sam seemed to be absorbing the beauty of this ancient land.

This is the island of Ithaca, the home of the legendary Ulysses. Sailing home to his Kingdom Ulysses overcame the dooming song of the sirens by plugging his ears. He then came upon the six-headed monster Scylla who ate his crew, but Ulysses escaped and finally came home to Ithaca.

'Anna, he looks good today. I think the holiday will help him get well', said Yianni.

The next few days were chaotic—relatives and friends continually visiting the family home to greet their Australian cousins. Sam stayed in bed. The relatives asked questions. As the days passed Anna was increasingly disturbed by Sam's reluctance to come out of his bedroom and be part of the family. She thought Sam felt embarrassed because his grasp of the Greek language was not very good. But most of the family spoke to him in English.

Anna was afraid of village gossip. It would hurt Yianni. Eventually she and Sam went for a walk through the olive trees scattered around the property that had belonged to the Petropolis family for generations. It was then villagers noticed him walking. They remarked to Yianni that Sam seemed a quiet, respectable young man. Anna was pleased, buoyed up. The trip was working.

For the first two weeks Sam and Anna walked to the beach and swam in the little alcoves hidden behind large rocks and ate delicious summer fruits. Sam relaxed. Anna told him stories she'd heard from her mother. Sam began to ask questions. The holiday will cure my son, she thought. It's good. She was happy. When they returned to the village home Sam went to his bedroom. He reappeared hours later, talking to himself and shouting, 'Get out, get out.' His uncles just looked at each other and his father said, 'It's OK son.' That's all he said.

The heat intensified. Sam noticed some children playing near the church. He talked to them in English but his words made no sense. Later, when they saw him again, they would say the silly words. Sam was peaceful in the company of children; it was as if he wanted to be a child again.

Sam and Anna decided to go for a walk to the next village and asked Yianni to meet them in the city square about four in the afternoon. Lizards of all sizes rushed past the track and the buzz of the wasps was unsettling. They walked slowly on the rocky road amongst the olive trees. Sam wanted to sit by the trunk of an olive tree and drink water. Anna wished she hadn't agreed to walk to this village.

Sam kept moving away; he was talking to himself.

'You're not my mother', he screamed, 'I was born in outer space and the powers of outer space arranged for the loan of your womb for me to be born'. Anna froze.

Then slowly she unwound and started to explain his birth. She was his real mother, he was born at St Andrews hospital and Yianni was his father. Dr McKenzie delivered him in 1961.

She was so agitated. She talked loudly, explaining all the details of his birth. The more she tried to justify the truth the angrier Sam became. The look in his eyes was frightening. He started talking to himself and repeating, 'You're not my mother'. Anna stopped talking. She found a pack of cigarettes in her bag.

'Sam, here's a cigarette.' He grabbed the cigarette, lit it with trembling hands, puffed quickly while silently looking up at the sky.

They met Yianni in the village square. 'Anna, our boy looks good today', he said as he hugged her. Sam was calm and wanted to have coffee and ice cream. Anna decided not to tell Yianni about Sam's outburst.

In the evening the three of them enjoyed a home cooked meal. It was good; Anna was encouraged. Sam was calm and wanted to play cards with his father. He won each game and seemed happy with his success. He went to bed.

Nearly midnight and a scream pulled Yianni and Anna from their dreams. 'Get out.' It repeated over and over again. The screaming grew louder and louder. Anna and Yianni rushed into Sam's bedroom.

The neighbours heard the screams and gathered by the gate whispering, 'Call the doctor. Call the police.'

Sam stopped and started to cry. He wouldn't be touched. Anna and Yianni turned to one another and faced the awful truth. Sam was having a psychotic episode and this strange illness might never go away.

The next morning Sam came into the kitchen wanting breakfast as if nothing had happened the previous night.

The holiday was a mistake. They must fly home as quickly as possible. They left the island with much sadness. Anna and Yianni said goodbye to their relatives who couldn't grasp the complexities of schizophrenia and why such a nice young man should behave so bizarrely.

To reach Athens they had to catch two ferries. The first ferry left at 6 am and they worried if Sam would wake up in time. Anna gave Sam his night tablet in the afternoon hoping he would fall asleep earlier than usual. Sam wanted to return to Melbourne and go to Bendigo for his alarming need to gather feathers and stones.

Anna was frightened. They boarded the first ferry and Sam sat on the deck drinking coffee. He seemed calm as they reached the little port where they were to transfer to the second boat by walking over a plank placed between two boats.

'Dad I need cigarettes, look there is a small shop, I'll just run and buy a packet then join you on the second boat.'

They called Sam but he couldn't hear them. They lost sight of him. Where is Sam?

An old man who knew Yianni called to him, 'He's in the sea, swimming towards the wrong ferry'. Anna screamed and Yianni ran off to find the captain.

'Come to this boat', he yelled through the loud speaker. Anna held her breath. Sam was a strong swimmer. Other passengers also started calling for Sam to come to their ferry, others tried to comfort Anna, while Yianni fumbled with his clothes as if he might jump in the water to save Sam.

Sam raised his head, turned and gave a short salute. He'd heard Anna screaming.

It only took a few minutes for Sam to be dragged back onto the ferry. Anna rushed towards him and together with Yianni guided Sam below decks to change into dry clothes. As they walked Anna burned with embarrassment. Everyone knew. She felt as if she was marked with a sign:

See this woman. Look what she's done to her son.

It's this schizophrenia, it's ruined our lives. They don't understand. It's an illness.

She was so frustrated and confused. It took some time to find his bag. With tears streaming down her face she found a pair of jeans, a jumper, some undies and a pair of thongs.

At the port they were instructed to speak to the detective waiting to interview Sam. Maybe Sam was a drug courier. 'How ridiculous, Yianni said. The detective questioned Sam who gave him some vague answers. The more answers Sam gave to the detective's probing questions the more baffled the man became. Interrupting the farce about feathers and stones Yianni asked to speak to the detective's superior. It was over.

Anna found an understanding doctor who prescribed sleeping tablets so Sam would sleep for most of the trip home and not cause more trouble.

When they landed in Melbourne the effects of the tablets had not worn off. The customs officer asked Sam to stand aside so he could check him. Sam became agitated, talking loudly, mostly nonsense and pacing around. Yianni tried to explain to the customs officer. Anna kept asking Sam questions. 'What is wrong?' Everyone stared. Eventually the customs sniffer dog was brought in and started walking around Sam who was muttering something no one understood.

'OK no problems', shouted the customs officer, 'you can go home'. Home. The best word in the world.

Sam was very quiet. He had concluded that their holiday was a dream. Anna let his words slide. Who wants to remember a nightmare!

Weeks passed and Sam had some good days. His medication was changed but the bad days seemed to dominate. He thought his mother was poisoning him even though he'd asked her to cook his favourite dish.

Anna attended carer groups to understand how to manage Sam. Some things worked, others didn't. Yianni retreated to his music room and played mournful tunes, or he would spend hours nurturing his vegetables. It often seemed that he was looking for answers as he filled the basket with beans for the neighbours.

Sam yelled, 'Get out, get out', as he stood under the orange tree in the back garden watching his father tending his vegetables. Sam was really yelling at the voices that he could hear coming from outside his ears. Sometimes he screamed at night and would punch holes in the wall. Later he would clean up the mess; paste a picture of his favourite football team on the wall.

Life was difficult for Anna, for Yianni.

Sam wasn't taking his medication.

He was given a monthly injection. Although he wasn't happy he trusted his doctor.

Anna struggled to accept that life was different now; Sam would not be like he was before the illness. Sam was gone. It took Yianni longer.

One night Yianni noticed the light in Sam's room so he decided to say goodnight to him. He missed the close relationship he'd had with his son. The room was a mess; no mattress, a small table and chair missing and clothes everywhere. He asked what was going on. Sam replied he was leaving home. He knew what he was doing. Bewildered, Yianni called Anna. There was nothing they could do. Sam ignored them completely.

Reluctantly Yianni took Anna's hand and went back to bed. This wasn't the first time Sam was doing something strange.

The next morning Sam's room was bare. Sam had put the furniture, his mattress and clothes in the panel van and dumped them at the local opportunity shop.

Anna walked to the shop to retrieve the goods. The manager refused to return anything. She couldn't prove that they belonged to her, could she?

Anna argued; couldn't this woman understand her son was a very sick person? She wouldn't listen. Anna picked up the black and white jumper she'd given Sam for his birthday. She had bought the fleece, spun the wool on her spinning wheel and then knitted a complicated pattern. It was very special because the spinning and the knitting of this jumper was part of her recovery. She begged the lady to let her have it back.

'You can buy it for ten dollars', this cow of a woman said. Anna had left the house without her purse. She thought of yelling a string of vile Greek curses but she couldn't and turned to leave.

An elderly man holding a plastic bag called her. 'Here is the jumper for your son.' Anna thanked him profusely. There were still good people in the world.

Sam retreated within himself. His delusions about family were weird. He referred to them as ancient Gods: Zeus, Poseidon, Hermes and Hera.

He was admitted to hospital to be trialled on a new medication, Clozapine.

Seven days later Sam was allowed home. In the car Sam, still a little sleepy, was observing the environment. He started talking to Yianni.

'These buildings are magnificent. They are so high. I've never seen how green the trees are. It's great to breathe again.'

Yianni looked at his son and thought where has Sam been for the past twelve years?

When they arrived home Sam hugged Anna. She had waited so many years for this love. Tears flooded down her face. For the next month a special team visited Sam at home each day to monitor his progress. His doctor and case manager encouraged him to attend education programs. He began to smile.

On bad days some of the old symptoms reappeared. Those days worried Anna and Yianni. Tomorrow was never certain. Sam's case manager gave Anna support and some strategies on how to help Sam. She also started cognitive behaviour therapy with Sam, who responded well. Within two years Sam started working. Sam was now well. But was he?

Symptoms of anxiety surfaced at work. The machinery used in the clothing factory where he worked was complicated. He resigned, couldn't cope applying for another job. He joined a clubhouse where people with mental illness met. They had opportunities to learn basic skills and the opportunity of friendship. But Sam was always withdrawn and very quiet. Although he still experienced symptoms he was learning how to understand and manage.

Anna continued to be involved, working within the mental health system. Yianni spent more hours in his garden; so sad that Sam didn't want to play music with him. Yianni's unhappiness worried Anna.

Meanwhile, the Petropolos family grew. Great-grandchildren brought great joy to the family. Although Sam didn't show much emotion it was beautiful to see him greet his nieces and nephews in his own special way.

Yianni had a quadruple by-pass heart operation and was later diagnosed with a rare eye disease. How would Sam react? Anna was frightened. Would Sam suffer a relapse?

In July of that year, Yianni died. His life was celebrated with stories. His grandson played a song his grandfather often played. Sam, with the help of his clinicians, managed these events in a dignified way.

Years passed and Sam, now in his fifties was coping with his life, living with Anna who was still involved helping families.

Anna had at last come to understand that Sam had changed. He was Sam. This is Sam and no one else.

In October 2014 Sam welcomed all his family to his home. Yianni and Anna had planned to build a unit for Sam at the back of their home. Yianni would often tell her, 'Anna, our boy will manage his life when he is fifty'.

And so it was that on a Saturday, October 11 Sam moved into his new home. It was all his.

There was a family gathering with decorations placed on the windows of the new unit. A ribbon was tied across the back door. Watching Sam cut this ribbon Anna's heart soared. He looked so happy. He showed emotions that Anna hadn't seen for so many years. He gave a beautiful speech.

Anna will always remember the day Sam told her, 'Mum, there was a hole in my head and now it's gone. Mum, did you see the roses? They are beautiful.'

If only Yianni was with us.

So much of Anna's beautiful youngest son has been locked away by the complicated symptoms of schizophrenia. But today, in his own home, Sam is at peace.

About The Author

Kali Paxinos was born in Australia. Her parents migrated from Greece. She was the eldest of three girls. Her family followed the traditions and culture of the Greek community. An arranged marriage to Tatsi Paxinos in 1947 was a happy one and five children followed. Although absorbed with her growing family she became aware of many problems surfacing within the migrant population. As a bilingual speaker she spent many hours supporting young mothers attending maternity wards and the children's hospital, later helping them understand the education system. She was appointed a migrant teacher aide at a technical school where many migrant children had language problems. It was during these years that she was invited to speak to teachers about understanding cultural issues.

Kali was appointed a probation officer to work with children from migrant backgrounds. She helped adults with literacy problems. When her youngest son was diagnosed with schizophrenia she advocated for improvements to the mental health system. Her advocacy focused on problems within culturally and linguistically diverse groups. As a carer/consultant she supported families and spoke at conferences around Australia. She has been involved in teaching programs. The book *Shedding the Black Coat* by Jill Parris tells Kali's story.

LETTER TO AUSTRALIA

MOHAMMED ADNAN BHATTI

Dear Australia
Here are some things I'd like you to know:

Families in Pakistan
Respect and dignity is the foundation of the Pakistani family with each member proud to be part of this the central building block of our society.

We are proud to be known by our family and share everything in common. Usually our earnings go to the grandmother or mother who works as family treasurer and housekeeper. She has responsibility for home and to provide everything the family needs. Anyone in the family who needs something must approach her.

Even a new bride coming into the groom's family must follow her mother-in-law's instructions as her daughters do, so she must adjust more to her new family rather than her new husband. This is why some new brides become stressed and place demands on their husbands to provide a new home in which she can take charge of her own home in her own particular way.

The responsibility of the family resides with the grandfather. If he is in good health the power is his and the rest of the family operates under his leadership. If he is not in good health, the power is handed to his eldest son.

Since the women of the family hold its dignity, they have to be respected and honoured. In turn, they must respect their elders and must maintain their dignity by keeping away from bad things that may ruin the family's respect.

If a daughter has a boyfriend who is considered to be disrespectful of the family she could either be married to someone chosen against her will, or even killed as punishment. While marriages are arranged, the boys are at liberty to talk about and choose the girl they want to marry.

Each day starts with the Pakistani family going to church, the mosque, *Gadara*, or temple. Afterwards breakfast is taken to the fields where both men and women till the land. Farmers leave for work early in the morning and finish early to avoid the heat in summer. Breakfast is eaten at about ten o'clock in summer and noon in winter.

School-going children go to school. Men and women who work in offices leave at approximately the same time in the morning. Men eat two meals a day, but women and children have three. Dinner is eaten between five and six o'clock because there is no electricity. The rest of the family members help those working in the fields.

In summer this is how the day finishes: women and children sleep outside in the courtyard, while the men sleep in the fields with their dogs, watching over their livestock, smoking hookah and singing folk songs. Some farmers play the flute for recreation, while the women tell their children stories before they go to sleep.

How I came to Australia

My father motivated me to venture into a different society and culture to get my education from the people around me, rather than from a university. He heard that Australia is a multicultural country which could offer an environment where I could gain an understanding of how things are done in a progressive society.

We went to the Australian Consulate near the Faisal Mosque in Islamabad. I was accepted as a student because I had achieved good marks in my previous education. Everything was finalised and I came to Melbourne in July 2009.

The house in which I stayed when I arrived was strange to me because it was made of wood and had small rooms. The weather was also very surprising. The sun burned my arms, but I did not sweat; quite different from back home. I didn't know how to drive a car or cook my own food so my housemates gave me lessons.

At first Australia was a stressful and depressing country. I did not know, when I planned to come here, that I had committed myself and my family to paying thousands and thousands of dollars to the education industry.

Unfortunately this was only the beginning of my struggles. The colleges I attended were set up to get fees from students, but not to teach or provide an adequate education or even to give certificates at the end of years of study.

I had to find work because coming here had cost so much. I began a career in the security industry but found I was treated like a robot. Working helped me live and pay for my studies, but my employers took advantage of my insecurity and my lack of knowledge about my rights. They did not provide rosters. Even when we asked for days off they would call at two in the morning and demand our immediate response to any call. My bosses did not expect me to have any time off. There was simply no recognition that we might have a private life. I became angry and sorry for myself and for others who worked under such conditions.

But there is always good with the bad and I have found that most Australians have beautiful manners, are generous and are not violent. This country has a good education system and people do not have to wait in long lines to get medical treatment. Things are organised. In short, I like the system of government I see here.

In 2011 my brother joined me. I tried to transfer my positivity about this being a good place on to him. Some good things come from bad. On a day in the first week of October 2012 I got a four-hour shift at the Malthouse Theatre in Southbank. I didn't want to go because I had already worked a full shift during the day at the ANZ Bank, but my employer couldn't find anyone else so I went.

Here I met Komahi and his friend Lisa and this soon changed my mind about taking this shift. I had found my life partner and her cat, Sputnik. I began to court Lisa. We watched movies together, went out to dinner and did many other things. Eventually I met her parents. Then Lisa trusted me enough to take me camping. The world looked brighter after that: As if a rainbow had come out after a heavy storm.

We bought an old house together, demolished many walls and very soon after this we invited the builder in. Then we got married. Concerned about my work I began looking for a business to buy. Just to add a little spice, my new wife became pregnant immediately; we became the proud parents of a baby boy in March 2014. His name is Mika. He is a very cuddly and friendly little man. I love the excuse to behave like a young man again and so enjoy playing with his balloon and toys and sharing my music with him in the car.

Six months ago we bought a hairdressing saloon and now we both work in that business and share the care of our family.

I now see that our destinies were to meet and to grow together. I think our power has come from the many meals Lisa's parents cooked us in their home, even if I needed to add a lot of spice to meet my taste. I have grown to love in my mother's home.

My plans for the future are to do something good for humanity. I have wanted to do this from early childhood. I wish to help the children in my homeland get a good education and later, say when I'm about fifty, I want to go back to my country and teach general knowledge to these children. This I will do by telling stories from my life. I would also like to save enough money to renovate a school and build a computer library, but not until my children are mature enough to look after themselves.

My wife is amazing. She is helping me with the business and our home and looking after Mika. But most wonderful is that we think the same way and, most of the time, her parents support us in building a life together. Life is safe in Australia. You are allowed to practice any religion and no one will stop you.

I am looking forward to a bright future in this town.

My views on Politics in Pakistan

In Pakistan politics is only for the rich and uneducated. Poor qualified people can do nothing against politicians because they have no money to spend on election campaigns. The rich have made politics their business and get richer and richer and are less and less aware of the important issues like education, hospitals and infrastructure that affect the communities from which they come. They also do not like collecting taxes from their rich mates and do not care that these revenues could make a huge difference to the lives of the poor and needy.

Your average Pakistani citizen has little education and few resources, while many rich politicians enjoy using their wealth, power and high office in the National Assembly to undermine the poor. Corruption is rife, infrastructure is crumbling and government often misuses resources as politicians fall over each other to take the country back toward the Stone Age with no water, electricity, gas or even a roof over people's heads; so the rich get richer and the poor, poorer. Suicide is commonplace because the ordinary man cannot pay his household bills or his children's school fees.

Now slowly, slowly people are beginning to understand why their country is so far behind progressive countries.

My views on Politics in Australia

In Australia politics is not a business; it is a job. Most politicians are highly qualified and compete with each other to do the best for their community. It makes me thirsty and hungry when I see how good the education system, hospitals and infrastructure are. I long for such systems within my birth country.

One thing does worry me. When I turn on my television I notice that all the parliamentarians belong to the white community and all the television programs are translated into English, while when you look at Australian society itself it is not like this: There are people here from all over the world.

My wife tells me the real Australians are Aboriginals. It saddens me that Aboriginals do not enjoy the sweetest of what society here has to offer. They deserve this. They looked after Australia for thousands of years for all of us and we just desecrate their things and put them in museums for our enjoyment.

Politicians should consider them. I hope an Aboriginal will be prime minister one day, although I can see this won't happen for a long time.

Thanks for listening.
Your friend
Adnan

About The Author
I was born in Gujyana Nou, Sheikhupura in Punjab province of Pakistan in 1990. My grandfather's younger brother married a nurse who was my first teacher. She did not run a registered school, but ran a school for interested children in a parent's home and I began my schooling there. We moved into the city in 1996 and were tested for the local junior school. I was placed in first grade. After five years I went to the local high school from which I graduated. After that I went to the local government college and received my Year 12 FSC Level 12 Certificate of Science.

The army was recruiting. I applied and did some training in Lahore, was tested in Gujranwala but did not pass, so decided I would like to go to a university to study engineering. At the same time my father told me that he had arranged a fine start for me at a college in Australia.

Little did he know what would happen to me once I arrived in Melbourne in July 2009. Some friends from my home city in Pakistan fetched me from the airport and took me to Glenroy. Within a couple of weeks all my money was stolen. Thus began my time in Australia.

Later, when I was involved in the government roofing insulation project, I realised that there are many types of corruption in Australia and the lives of innocent people are put at risk.

VOICELESS JOURNEY

ELHAM SHAHHOSEINI

In July 2012, after ten months in Melbourne, Sara and her son Pooya were returning to their homeland Iran to visit their family and Ali; Sara's husband and Pooya's father. When they finally landed at Imam Khomeini Airport in Tehran, the capital of Iran, they were excited and joyful.

Travelling from the middle of winter into the middle of summer is odd. But as a woman in Iran where the Islamic hijab (a scarf on your head and a long tunic and pants on your body) is compulsory, the middle of summer is an uncomfortable time of year. But even the annoying clothes and worse, the ideological regime which imposes these rules, could not spoil Sara's happiness.

As they left the plane Tehran's hot air touched their faces as if to say, 'Welcome home'.

After twenty hours of flight they were naturally quite exhausted, but the elation of seeing the people they loved made them forget about their tiredness. Emerging from Customs and Immigration Sara could see her mother and father but no Ali. Where was Ali? Sara saw the same question on Pooya's face: where was his father?

After the kissing and the hugs Sara demanded to know where Ali was. Her parents did not know. Her dad tried to calm them. 'He may be busy with his work in Yazd. I am sure he will contact us very soon', he said. There was a long silence and it seemed to Sara that everybody had somehow agreed not to mention Ali again.

While Sara was used to Ali's absences; his job required him to travel so frequently and widely they even had a comic name for him, 'Marco Polo'; this time something in her heart kept telling her, Something is wrong.

Homecoming
Sara's homecoming was uneasy. Her mum missed Sara and her grandson, fifteen year old Pooya, and she nagged Sara because she was unhappy. Sara could never understand why her mother couldn't accept they had to leave Iran to make a better life and future for Pooya in a free country, where no one could be arrested because of his religion or beliefs. She had been denied that chance to grow up in freedom; her life, happiness, childhood and adolescence were sacrificed to the Islamic republic and war. Her mum had tasted the bitterness of fear and hatred. Did she really want her daughter and grandson to stay in this stifling atmosphere?

Unbidden her memories marched before her eyes; she turned inwards and lost sight of her family.

Her mum's younger brother, her dear uncle, had been arrested shortly after the Islamic revolution. She remembered that very dark time when he was imprisoned for his political opinions; he was a socialist and was sentenced to fifteen years in prison. How could she forget those grey Tuesdays when she and her mum used to visit him regularly in Rajai-shahrJail in Karaj? Those days never left her mind. They had to wear the chador (a long black hijab) and wait for a long time while enduring the insults of the jail's guards. In the final year of the war between Iran and Iraq, in the summer of1988 just a couple of months before the end of the war, the Islamic regime decided to rid itself of more than 5000 political prisoners forever; quickly and secretly and in just one week. She never forgot that painful Tuesday when she was just sixteen. She and her mum were on their regular visit, but instead of the guard taking them to see her uncle the guards handed them his clothes and said to her mum that her brother had been executed two days ago. That long ago image returned. She could see everything in silent slow motion: her mum falling in a faint to the floor, herself shocked and crying...

'Sara', someone called. She blinked, found herself still standing at the airport in Tehran surrounded by her family in 2012.

'Sorry', she said.

'Are you all right? I think you are very tired', her mum said.

'I am okay. Let's go home', she said.

Summonsed

Sara was thinking, *What am I doing here, seated in a long room waiting for someone to call my name? What am I doing here, in a court in Tehran?* Just the day before, after spending three happy days with her family in the country, she had returned to her apartment in Tehran to find a piece of paper, a summons ordering her to appear in court.

At first she wondered what she had done wrong to be summonsed, but she knew—*Oh, poor Sara, you don't need to do anything 'wrong' to be summonsed to a court in Iran*—and was terrified.

After four hours of waiting her heart sank as two huge bearded men approached. Their faces were like those who had arrested the protesters of the Green Movement on the streets in 2009; like those who had questioned her in 2007 about her Sufism beliefs. Sufism. Her beloved Sufism, a mystical approach to Islam emphasising meditation over prayer. Classical Sufi scholars defined Sufism as, 'A science whose objective is the reparation of the heart and turning it away from all else but God'. The Sufi teacher, Ahmad ibn Ajiba, defined it as, 'A science through which one can know how to travel into the presence of the Divine, purify one's inner self from filth, and beautify it with a variety of praiseworthy traits'. Such a harmless and peaceful spiritual activity can cause serious trouble in Iran. Such a basic human right was a big issue for the Islamic government. Article 18 of the Universal Declaration of Human Rights states, 'Everyone has the right to freedom of thought, conscience and religion', but it is no more than a joke in Iran.

As they drew closer to her she felt not only terror but also hatred…

Before they even called her name she stood, knowing she would be insulted and questioned again, but this time they had a surprise for her; she would not be investigated here in this place. They ordered her to follow them; they would take her to an unknown place in a van…

As she sat in the windowless van an avalanche of jumbled thoughts passed through her head and she tried over and over to work out just what she had done or not done that threatened the government. So, she had become a member of a Sufist group and used to attend their weekly gatherings regularly. Even now, confined in a windowless van to nowhere, she could not suppress her smile as she recalled the almost inexpressible honour she felt at having being accepted into the group; she had been searching for the true meaning of life, love and humanity for many years and at last could find her answers, and this had raised her confidence. But just five years earlier she had paid a high price for her beliefs; she could clearly remember the day she was interrupted at work when someone from the security department called asking her to come to the interview room where someone from the National Intelligence Service wanted to see her. Under escort, she saw that even the security guards were frightened. In the office meeting room she endured long hours of aggressive and rude questioning about her most private beliefs. It had been a terrible experience. Eventually, she had been compelled to sign a declaration saying she would not attend Sufist gatherings in future, despite knowing it was all lies. She had certainly not been convinced by their admonitions that Sufism is against Allah and against Islam, or that a Sufi is an enemy of God. My God!

She felt the van slowing and her thoughts jerked to the present. Wherever they were, they were here.

Interrogation

Sara woke in the middle of night. At first she could not remember where she was. For a microsecond she thought it had been a nightmare, that it was all a dream, but then she recalled the events of the last three days and began to cry. This was her third day in this ugly, filthy basement in an unknown place. She had been questioned about Ali's life, his beliefs and where he was hiding. She had no idea where he was.

Her guards had the keys to her apartment and searched it thoroughly. Now Sara realised that she was in a big trouble, because almost every single activity in her daily life was illegal from the Islamic government's point of view—the books she read, the drinks she enjoyed, the movies she watched, the satellite TV channels she viewed—and now everything was revealed. They found her Sufist books, Ali's hand scripts about the book he was trying to publish, the satellite receiver and the alcoholic drinks. Apparently, he and his friends had tried to translate and publish some books about the history of Iran; obviously not the government's version.

That's why the previous day they had told Sara, 'You are in big trouble', that's why they insulted her and said bad words to her about her family, that's why she had lost her temper and argued with them, and that's why they had slapped her and threatened her and her son with…

Shivering with the cold, worried about her family and her son, she stopped crying. What was happening to her family? She did not know where they were or what they were doing. She paced the small room; back and forth, back and forth; unable to sleep, her brain churning, her entire life alive before her eyes.

Her childhood before the Islamic revolution was short, but all pictures captured in her mind were colourful and happy. Then, within a year of the Revolution in 1979, she had become a little woman; learning about war, death, execution, sanctions, coupons for almost everything, even lollies. At the age of seven she was considered mature enough to wear the Hijab! Not only Sara, but also all her friends at school, had never before encountered that black piece of fabric they now had to wear everywhere. Almost every morning for eight years, during the war between Iran and Iraq, Sara woke to the sound of military music and marches playing from her dad's radio. Every TV programme supported the war and the viewpoints of the Islamic government towards war and enemies. Soon fed up with the propaganda, although she had no access to independent media, she realised the Islamic government's ideology was bad and that thousands of thinkers and activists like her uncle were in jail or had been killed by the government. At sixteen she had seen the merciless and brutal face of the Islamic regime when her uncle was executed in secret at the prison...

When she heard footsteps approaching Sara broke off her reverie and wiped her face; crying in front of the guards was the last thing she wanted. She thought, Your Islamic regime has destroyed my life, what more do you want from me?

Escape
Flying had always been exciting for Sara, but this time was quite different: she was hopeful she would be allowed to leave, terrified that she would be held, and immensely sad to leave her parents knowing she would never be allowed to return. During the long drive to the Imam Khomeini International Airport she said nothing, was silent. That she was out of that hellhole jail was a miracle; her father had spared no effort to find out where she was being held and after three days of searching, even in morgues, and with the assistance of a lawyer, he rescued Sara from the detention. She paid a big bond to be free and was given only two weeks to appear again in court. She was told her name had been placed on a black list and if she tried to leave Iran, as soon as she showed her passport she would be arrested at the airport. There was a way to get out of Iran without having her passport checked, but it would cost a lot. She had never imagined that one day she would have to sell her jewellery for a bribe! Had never imagined that one day she would happily handover all her savings and jewellery to flee her homeland. She never imagined that one day she would be forced to leave her homeland forever...

Sara and Pooya sat waiting at the airport. They had been told not to check-in their luggage until the very last announcement. Now their lives and destiny were held in the hands of one airport guard who had been paid the bribe. Sara was well aware of the risks of paying a bribe, but she also knew that if she stayed an even worse future lay before her: Pooya's future would be uncertain and he would always be under suspicion, while she would be subject to frequent detention, questioning and imprisonment. Ali had disappeared, her apartment sold for the bond, all her savings and valuable possessions gone for the bribe.

She kept her head down and wondered how many other faces had been kept down in airports, waiting to flee Iran, during the last thirty-five years? How many other thinkers, activists, journalists, liberals, writers, poets and dissidents had already fled? How many other families and marriages had the Islamic regime destroyed? How long would it take to see a free Iran?

Sara could guess answers to all but the last of the questions.

Sara had been instructed to wait until the last announcement; but the wait for that announcement seemed interminable and she would never forget a single second of it, terrified they would be caught by the airport guards or the police, or worse, the plane would leave without them. A man came up to them and ordered them to follow him. Sara took her son's hand firmly and did not dare to raise her head. They almost had to run to keep up with the man. Just for a moment she looked sideways at Pooya's face and saw it was as pale as a sheet of paper, she guessed her own was no better.

Even after several hours of flight Sara was still a bundle of nerves. How had it happened? Numb, she felt numb; during that frantic dash to the plane, could remember only the moment they reached the airplane door and it had seemed everyone else was waiting for them because no sooner had they stepped aboard, than the door of the plane closed behind them.

Sara and Pooya were seated quickly. The aircraft taxied and took off. Sara looked out the tiny window and kept watch until the clouds blocked all sight of the land below. She knew that it was almost certainly her last chance to see her homeland: from now, Iran would be visible only in pictures and news on her computer screen.

About The Author
Elham Shahhoseini came to Australia with her son in 2011, seeking protection due to the extreme political and religious situation in her homeland of Iran.

In her homeland Elham worked as a researcher and university lecturer. In her first few years in Australia Elham was unable to apply for paid work due to visa restrictions, so she volunteered at a refugee centre teaching other women sewing skills. It was through the Ecumenical Migration Centre of the Brotherhood of St. Laurence that she became a member of the writing group. She has written short stories and poems in her mother language, Persian, and in the writing group she was encouraged to write in English. Elham wrote her first short story Silent Journey with the help of one of the writing group's mentors, Ian. This story reflects some of the major historical changes in her country from her point of view.

Elham was granted Australian permanent residency in 2014. She has recently been accepted into a local university to further her studies, and her son has just started his university degree.

ARE WE AT PEACE WITH OUR NAMES?

YUSUF SHEIKH OMAR

'What is your name?' she asked me with a big smile.
'Yusuf', I responded.
'Josef', she said, cupping her earlobe in an attempt to capture the way I pronounced it.
'Yusuf', I repeated.
'Yusuf', she said.
'Whatever is easy for you', I answered.

Though my name is one of the shortest and easiest to pronounce, I frequently encounter such questions at one of my favourite coffee shops in Fitzroy. People flock here in their morning break like thirsty camels around a water wheel in a desert land. 'Josef, Yusuf' is my everyday experience when interacting with the mainstream. I have to concede that I embarrassingly have also mispronounced the names of others. I remember how long it took me to say properly the name of my Sri Lankan friend, Rajalingam; and I am still reeling at some friends' names.

'Name' is more than a 'word'. It is a definition of person. It shapes your personality. Giving a name to a person is not an accident, but a cultural process: an historical, religious and social product. Some people are named after their grandmothers, grandfathers, cousins, aunts, uncles, national heroes or historical figures to keep generations connected. In the Somali culture some are named after an event such as *Geedi* (traveller) for someone born during travel or *Ubax* (flower) referring to someone born in a pleasing environment surrounded by aromatic flowers. In the Muslim world, all Mohameds are named after the Prophet Muhammad. I assume that other cultures and faiths have their own role-modelling names.

People change their names for various reasons. Social change posed by migration is one reason to adjust names. Resettlement and cultural adaptation in a new land affects our daily lives, including our names, attitudes and worldviews.

Believe me, a large number of Somalis in Australia have changed their names. 'Why do they do this?' you ask. The brutal and prolonged civil war has forced many to flee from death and resort to any means possible to survive, like being smuggled to a place where they can find protection and a better life. There have been rumours in the global Somali community that if newly arrived Somali refugees kept their actual names, destination governments could trace their travel route and return these people to their last country of departure. Because of this fear many change their real names as soon they arrive at Australian airports. Many still use these bogus names in official documents, but use their real names in the community. When I asked a friend of mine, 'Why don't you change back to your genuine name?' he responded, 'Too much paperwork. On every form, they ask you to write your previous names. I can't'.

Somalis are a nomadic and oral society. They enjoy travelling and talking, but not writing and reading. Some of the first generation who changed their true names have passed away, leaving their children with unknown family and clan names. These innocent young people are in limbo in the Somali community in Australia and in their country of origin. They often hear these insulting words: You have a fake family name.

When others return to Australia after travelling back to Somalia for cultural rehabilitation, they tell heartbreaking stories about relentless teasing, being accused of being false people, and some are disowned by their clans. Names may cause identity crises when interacting with the wider Australian community and make many lives difficult.

Once I went to an interstate conference. I met a young Somali-Australian woman. 'What is your name?' I asked.

'Sulaiykha or Sue in its short form', she answered.

'Which one do you prefer?' I asked.

She shrugged, saying: 'It depends where I am. In the Somali community I am Sulaiykha, in the mainstream I am Sue. It is very hard for Australians to say Sulaiykha. For Somalis it is Sulaiykha definitely. No Sue, no Sue for them. White people do the same: Liz is Elizabeth, Andy is Andrew and the list goes on'.

The other day I was at a multicultural youth meeting in the inner city of Melbourne. There was a young man name-tagged 'Moe'. After the meeting I chatted with him in the corner, calling him Moe.

'You can call me by my real name Mohamed' he said.

'So why Moe?' I asked.

'Just to fit with my friends and with the Aussies, you know', he said, 'otherwise you feel like an outsider plus you can't get a job with the name Mohamed'.

Academics have proved Moe's claim. If you have an original African, Asian, or Middle Eastern name, your chance of being called for an interview is six times less than if your name sounds Anglo-Saxon and you are a Smith or Kate. In the landscape of multicultural Australia, names that are easy to pronounce by the mainstream population are given more opportunities. They are also judged more positively than difficult to pronounce names like Al-Utaibi (Middle Eastern), ADEKAnMBI (Nigerian), Malakooti (Afghan), Etsehiwot (Ethiopian), Chenguang (Chinese). Research finds that even amongst Anglo-Saxon names, those with easily pronounceable names occupy higher status positions in big and prestigious law firms, court institutions or politics. Lucky you, Tony Abbott and Bill Shorten. Those with African, Asian, or Middle Eastern names are less likely to get a call back for a job interview or be promoted.

Australia is seen as a successful model of multiculturalism; however, this subtle and soft discrimination based on name profiling is chronic and growing in the Australian labour market, particularly at professional levels. It is slowly killing the ambitions and aspirations of many young migrants and refugees and competent Australians with unusual names.

Another issue linked to changing names is religious. On one occasion at a La Trobe University prayer room, I met an older Anglo-Saxon Muslim man.

'*Assalamu alaykum*' I greeted.

'*Wa'alaykum assalam*' he responded, as Muslim custom requires.

'What is your name brother?' I asked.

'Ahmed' he answered. 'I converted to Islam 30 years ago' he continued. 'I tell you, some new converts to Islam even change their family names believing this is true Islam. This is at odds with my understanding. I was taught this, and respected Islamic Scholars at the International Islamic University of Malaysia and traditional Somali *Fugahaa* (experts on Islamic jurisprudence) confirm it. Earlier in my life a well-respected local Somali Sheikh said, 'Prophet Muhammad never changed the names of new converts to Islam in his lifetime, unless the name had bad meaning within Islam. "Abdushamsi" (the slave of sun) is one such name. Almost all his companions kept their traditional names before they embraced Islam like Abubakar, Omar, Khadijo, Maria, Salman, Bilal, Suhayb and so on'. Even his own name 'Mohammad' was given to him 40 years before he became a prophet.

I often see new Muslims changing their original names from John or Janet to Osman or Aisha, and while I respect their choice I argue this has nothing to do with Islamic teachings. In the best cases I think it is drawn from Sheikh Google *Fatwaa* and not more than that. If anyone is going to change his or her name, I would invite the person to adopt an Australian aboriginal name. I think this is fair. My nickname will be Yahbini (star) from now on.

Christianity also looks on the same page. One day I had a sideline chat with a scholar of Christianity at an interfaith forum. We talked about the issue of changing names for religious purposes. He explained how many Africans and Asians changed their indigenous names during the missionary expansion in the 18th, 19th and early 20th centuries. He also told me about recently converted people to Christianity who changed their original

African and Asian names to Western look-alike names like James and Joanne. He wished they had kept their traditional names.

This reminds me of my own experience when I was new in Australia 13 years ago and went to an office. 'What is your Christian name?' asked an old lady filling out a form for me. Incensed and provoked I said, 'I am not Christian. I am Muslim,' defending my Islamic name identity in a religious battlefield on names.

'Oh, what is your name?' she retreated.

'Yusuf', I said, feeling a winner.

Changing names can also involve security issues. We know most criminals, terrorists, wanted people, and Internet and social media pirates use anonymous names, so there is a good reason for asking when filling out important governmental forms if someone has been known by other names.

Names symbolise individual experiences, social values, norms, relationships and sometimes ethnicity and status in societies. When you change your name, you remove all these important connections to personal history, social memories and belonging to your original community. This could lead to an identity crisis, social disconnection, loss of networks, ambivalent personality, emotional disturbance and psychological instability to the point where the person could become like an uprooted tree, blown about and flung to a remote and distant land.

Australia is a free society. Everyone is entitled to choose whatever religion, lifestyle and name they wish. Such freedom however should be used wisely, because changing names may have undesired consequences at the individual and community levels. And the question to ask ourselves is, just because it is easy, should we do so?

About The Author

Dr Yusuf Sheikh Omar earned his PhD in refugee studies from La Trobe University in 2011 with his dissertation: Integration From Youths' Perspectives: A Comparative Study of Young Somali Men in Melbourne (Australia) and Minneapolis (USA); Masters of Educational Leadership and Management from La Trobe University, Australia; a second Master of Human Science (Teaching Arabic as a Second Language) from International Islamic University, Malaysia; Bachelor of Education from International University of Africa, Sudan; and numerous diplomas including a diploma in Conflict Prevention, Management, Resolution and Peace Building from the International Peace and Security Institute, based in Washington DC, in partnership with John Hopkins University (Italy); and a Certificate IV in Training and Assessment from Victoria University, Australia.

Yusuf has taught at Victoria and La Trobe Universities and worked as a researcher at the University of Melbourne and Victorian Transcultural Mental Health, St Vincent's Hospital. He has published widely in national and international academic journals as well as in the leading Australian newspapers including *The Age* and *The Sydney Morning Herald*.

Yusuf is a writer, a poet and a peace activist and is passionate about justice for refugees, asylum seekers and people in difficult situations e.g. displaced people and those living in war-torn countries. He was a former member of the African Ministerial Consultative Committee for the Australian Federal Government (2012-2013). He is also an independent consultant on intercultural and forced migration issues. Yusuf is the founder and first president of the Somali Australian Friendship Association, an active member of African Think Tank, a board member of the External Education Advisory Group of Victoria Police, a board member of the Victorian Cooperative on Children's Services for Ethnic Groups (VICSEG), a member of the Community Leader Reference Group at the Department of Immigration and Border Protection, a former panel member of the Refugee Scholarship Committee of the Department of Justice, Victoria, and a former board member of the Austin Hospital Community Advisory Committee. Since 2010, Yusuf has been organising annual African graduation ceremonies at the Parliament House of Victoria.

Yusuf has received numerous awards including: 'Ambassador for Peace', The Universal Peace Federation (2013); 'Banyule Community Volunteer Award', Banyule City Council (2011); 'Spectrum Seeds for Growth', Spectrum Migrant Resource Centre (2010); 'Refugee Award' from the Equality and Diversity Centre, La Trobe University (2010); 'Outstanding Service to the Community', Parliament of Victoria (2008); 'Victorian Refugee Recognition Record', Victorian Multicultural Commission held at Immigration Museum, Melbourne (2005); 'Australia Day Award, 'Service Above Self', Rotary Club Of Rosanna, Melbourne, (2005).

A CHAPTER FROM RAISED IN CONFLICT

ESSAN DILERI

Thursday night was usually great because my parents came home from work mid-afternoon and Mum would prepare a special meal of Afghan delicacies. I would go to school in the afternoon and finish at five. This Thursday I could not wait to finish school because there was soccer against a team from Kocha-e-Dash from the street behind our house. We were excited. They had challenged us,

'We are going to win.'

Saqeb, my best friend and the captain of our team was in good form. Everyone listened. We knew it was important.

When the ball fell into the street gutter filled with grey water it was called out. That day I retrieved the ball from it at least a dozen times without worrying about hygiene. I knew I had to focus fully on my play.

Neighbours were not happy about the match because we were very noisy. The street was the only place to have our matches as there were no parks or playgrounds in which we could play. The match would stop as a car passed through. During the first half we played hard and scored a goal. The second half was dramatic because the other team equalised. This meant we needed to work harder.

Saqeb kept hollering out the strategy and we focused. Khalil saved us in the last five minutes. We got another goal. Ecstatic we rushed to the mosque and gulped down water from the only available tap in our street and washed our hands and sweaty faces. We kept bragging about our win. Saqeb took us all to a milk shop where we enjoyed hot milk and *roat* (a round soft sweet bread).

Thursday was the only night that there were movies on the television and we all discussed what would be on that night. We rushed to the electrical junction and asked if it was our turn to get power. We were in luck. The operator said this Thursday was our turn so I rushed home.

As I got closer I could smell the *bolani* (a special Afghan dish), my favourite. Mum was the best cook. We ate it with yogurt mixed with cucumber and dried mint.

While we ate I spoke to my sisters about the match. Nahid, my oldest sister, wasn't so interested because we were noisy during the game. Zakia said well done and Shakeba my smallest sister just continued eating.

Dad said, 'Time to eat. You can talk about your game when you have finished'.

I couldn't wait for the power to come on at 8.30 pm and everyone cheered as the lights came up.

'Yes we will see the movie tonight!'

We knew that we would have to sit through the boring government reports before the movie began so we kept washing our faces with cold water to help us stay awake. Finally, at 9.30 pm *Murch Masala* started.

This movie was a grave disappointment because there was none of the action and fighting that excited me. Long and tedious, the film had not one action scene. Tired from the day's exploits I fell asleep before the movie ended.

I was in a deep sleep when a loud bang woke me. I looked around and soon saw Mum and Dad at the west window. My sister Zakia woke in shock.

The explosions got louder and closer. Dad took the ladder and climbed onto the roof to see what was going on and I followed. Red, green, orange and yellow explosions lit the western sky. The noise got closer and intensified. The smell of smoke filled the air. I could taste sulphur and the ground shook. I looked around to see neighbours on each roof. All faced west.

Children cried and whimpered and the adults shrieked and yelled.

'God help us!'

I became more and more afraid. It felt like the bombs were exploding on our street.

Dad climbed down and called us all inside. The windows trembled with each explosion. My heart raced and my mouth was dry. My little sister Shakeba cried and Mum soothed her but also cried out.

'*Khair Khudaya*' (God bless us).

The fire trucks shrieked as they rushed towards Qargha (the suburb where the ammunition depot was located) and my aunt and uncle rushed in. Their faces were filled with fear. Their house was right next to the ammo dump and they had run for their lives as their windows shattered and the roof began to fall on them.

The explosions continued and the noise raged for many hours but the night grew darker with only an occasional burst of light to the west. At 4.30 am we were still aware of the noise. By 5.30 am it was quiet except for the occasional ambulance or fire truck siren in the distance.

Our house was full and there was nowhere to sleep, which was fine by me. My heart was still pounding and I was too afraid to sleep. As the sun rose on Friday, our day of rest, we huddled together and talked about what had happened.

Later we went to my uncle's house to find all the windows shattered. Everything was covered in dust and it smelled of sulphur. It was still and deserted. People all looked on from a distance.

On Saturday morning before dawn I was woken from the sweetest sleep by the squeak of Russian tanks and trucks carrying ammo back to Qargha depot.

I was eight years old and will never forget the intensity of joy at winning at soccer, nor the extreme fear of the night that followed.

HOME TRUTHS

I grew up in beautiful Dehnaw Dehbori, a suburb of Kabul. It had tarred roads and our house was only a five minute walk from Kabul University. There were two double storied houses in our street, one built in the European style of Koti. I always dreamed of building one just like it.

My next-door neighbour made kites and I would watch as he prepared the string for flying them. To prepare the kite string he took thin thread and coated it with finely crushed glass and a sticky substance. I loved kite flying.

Two doors away lived our literature teacher. Her husband was very hard on us. When we sat on the concrete pavement in front of his house he would chase us yelling, 'You are messing my path'.

Down our road was a small shop that sold groceries. It was here that we would gather to chat and swap stories after school. We would tie a string to a ten Afghanis note, cover the string with dirt and wait across the street. If someone bent to pick it up we would tug on the string and laugh.

Another hangout, particularly in winter, was the electric circuit box, a hot spot that we would enjoy warming our hands against during cold sunny winter days.

Across from our house was a big pine tree. Its branches came over the wall and shaded the pavement. We would sit below it and chat in the cool breeze and pick nuts from the tree. These were very small and it was a lot of work to get them out of their shells but they were very tasty. Under the tree was a telephone pole about three and a half metres tall and we would compete to see who could climb the highest and get down most quickly. Saqeb was unbeatable.

One day Saqeb's dad caught him climbing the pole. He swore, grabbed Saqeb by the ear and yelled, 'Get home this minute.'

We did not see him again for the rest of that day. Being kept at home was a grave punishment because our only pastime was to play on the street.

The telephone line would break when we hit it with a ball and this would get us into trouble with one or another of our cranky neighbours. One day, while playing soccer on the street, I shot the ball and broke the line. Our neighbour's son told his dad who ran after me and took me home to my mum. I was so afraid that I started crying. I didn't want Dad to know. The cruel neighbour came over that evening, knocked on our door and spoke to Dad. He came back inside, furious, and smacked my bottom. I was banned from playing soccer in the street. I loved soccer so much that it almost broke my heart.

Eventually I played again. The telephone line was often broken.

About the Author

Essan Dileri was born in Kabul Afghanistan. He lives in Melbourne with his wife and children. He currently works as Programs Coordinator, Settlement and Family Services at Spectrum Migrant Resource Centre. He completed his MA in International Development in Ireland and has worked in international development and the community sectors for 13 years.

He came to Australia for the Parliament of World's Religions in Dec 2009 to present his work, but was not able to return and sought asylum in Australia.

He is the winner of the prestigious Refugee Recognition Record Award in 2011 and has recently published a book, *Raised in Conflict*, sharing first hand tales of conflict from his country Afghanistan. He is a strong and passionate advocate for refugees and asylum seekers.

He is a diehard supporter of the Collingwood Football Club.

MOVED TO MELBOURNE

NIKA SUWARSIH

I married my husband in January 2006 in Indonesia, and then I applied for a spouse visa to come to Australia. I came to Melbourne Australia in January 2007. I'm so happy to have moved to Melbourne because I will now always be close to my husband and we are re-united, but I am also sad because I am far from my family and friends in Indonesia.

At the Melbourne airport we drove our car to our new home in Clayton. At first this meant we would live and rent a room in our uncle's house. On the way to his home my husband drove the car and I sat beside him. I felt so happy with my husband and felt like the world belongs to us only. I liked the weather that is so fresh and clear. But sometimes as the days went on I still felt cold. I find that I can't handle cold in Melbourne.

When we arrived in Clayton we felt so happy that we had a nice bedroom for us, although without air conditioning. We paid rent of $600 a month for this room. My aunt was very kind and always cooked delicious food for us to eat.

As time went on we had some good days and some not so good days. Every day I must learn to adapt to my new situation. My husband worked nightshift from 9 pm to 8 am, so every night I slept alone without my husband. I was sad but we could still talk on the phone when he went to work.

At first I was very lonely and homesick living in Melbourne. I had no friends and not enough money because I didn't have work, I was bored with no activity and I just stayed home. I struggled with the language and I felt isolated because I didn't know where to go.

One day, still in January 2007, I didn't menstruate. I took a pregnancy test and the test was positive. Unbelievable. My first pregnancy! We made an appointment with our family doctor close to home in Clayton. The doctor said 'Congratulations, you are pregnant'. I was so happy and said thanks to God for my first pregnancy.

For the first three months I was very ill with morning sickness and vomiting every time I ate and drank. I couldn't eat at all and I couldn't drink like usual and I had to take bed rest. I was very weak. I had to go to hospital for three days because I had very bad pain in my stomach and I just couldn't handle it. The doctor even gave me morphine injections.

After that I had regular check-ups with the doctor for the rest of my pregnancy as well as ultrasounds. After three months I started to feel better and began to join the English study class every day, Monday to Friday from 9am to1pm. Joining the English classes helped improve my English and I also got new friends who are from multicultural backgrounds.

On the 15th of May 2007, on my birthday, I was five months pregnant. I was having my regular check up with the doctor in hospital. The ultrasound team announced to me that my baby may have Down syndrome. The team told me this is because the ultrasound shows the baby has got a big neck. The ultrasound team coordinator said to me, 'I will give you five minutes to make the decision if you want to take the blood test for Down syndrome which involves taking blood from the baby. I only have time to help you today'.

I had heard that taking blood from the baby would cause a miscarriage and I was already five months pregnant. I didn't want to lose my baby. I saw from the ultrasound he was so handsome and he had a nice nose. I said to her, 'Please give me time to think and make decisions. I can't make decisions in this short time. I need to go home and think and discuss this with my family'.

'Ok' she said. 'I will give you more time. I'll give you fifteen minutes to think and I will be back to you, otherwise next week

I will go to overseas so I can only help you today'. She went to her room and let me think for fifteen minutes, not enough for me to think. I just cried and cried, on my birthday. I got such bad news. If my baby had Down syndrome it would be unbelievable. Oh God help me and my baby to be healthy.

After fifteen minutes she came back to me. She asked me if I was ready. I said no, that I wanted to go home and think and that I will make decisions tomorrow or after three days. Then she let me go home.

I went home and cried. In my room I was still crying and I prayed to God to give me strength and health for me and my baby. All the time I prayed to God for a miracle. I called my counsellor for some help with my situation. After talking to her for a while, I felt a bit better and I was ready to talk with all my family about my situation.

I tried to read information about Down syndrome. What is Down syndrome? It was very helpful.

After three very difficult days I called the ultrasound team. My husband and I took the decision we didn't want to take blood from my baby, so we stopped the test for Down syndrome. I don't want a miscarriage in my first pregnancy. I continued to have regular check-ups for my pregnancy. I told the doctor that I stopped the Down syndrome blood test because I wanted to save my baby. I was already five months into my pregnancy. The doctor said to us that it was good and it was your choice.

From January onwards I still felt sad and lonely. I felt stressed to be so far from family. We communicated with them by phone and SMS. Sometimes I miss my mum and miss my friends and miss my country so much. I try to make my day as busy as possible and study every day and this makes me happier. Sometimes I feel the stress of my situation very much and I feel bored in Melbourne, homesick and lonely. When I feel like this I pray to God, Dzikir, and talk to God, practice relaxation, do meditation and singing. I walk and exercise, enjoy laughter therapy, join community activities, do some writing and reading to learn something new, make new friends, and talk to someone, talk to friends or family and also talk to the counsellor. This is very helpful to manage our very stressful situation.

After six months we moved to a new house where we still rent. We knew we would need more space if I delivered the baby so we found a nice three bedroom unit to rent. We moved from Clayton to Dandenong and I also moved for English classes. I was happy when I studied and learnt something new. I studied until the delivery of my baby on the 3rd of September 2007. In the morning I got a little blood on my pads. I still felt fine and studied as usual. During the day when I was still in class I got a call from the hospital telling me I needed to deliver my baby today because I had got blood on my pads.

At 2 pm my husband and I went to the hospital. I took the pads with blood on them with me and also some clothes. I felt fine and I didn't feel pain in my stomach. The doctor said to me because I had blood on my pads I needed to deliver the baby today.

Finally on the 4th of September 2007, at 4.30 am, I had a normal delivery in hospital. I had a new baby boy who was handsome and healthy. Thanks to God for this miracle. My baby didn't have Down syndrome. My baby was very healthy. Thank you Allah. Thank you for everything that you have done for me. I'm very happy because everything is good and blessed. To be continued…

NIKA'S SONGS OF HAPPINESS

Thank You Allah (Loving Me)
When I feel sad, you always make me happy
When I feel alone, you always come to me
When I feel weak, you are always close to me
When I need support, you are always helping me
You are the only one, can always help me
You are the only one, can always support me
You are the only one, can understand me
You are the only one, can do anything for me

Thank you Allah, thank you for everything
Thank you Allah, thank you for looking after me
Thank you Allah, thank you for anything
Thank you Allah, thank you for loving me.

You are my everything (You are the one)
I should come to you
Because you are very close to me
I love you and I need you
Please come to me

Guiding me all the way
Because I love your way
Blessing me all the way
Because I need your love

You are my destiny
You are the one (you are the only one)
You are my everything
You are the one (you are the only one)
In my life forever

Stop Anger
Stop anger, go anger
Keep smiling keep smiling
Stop anger go anger
Let us sing together

Stop anger, go anger
I'm happy You're happy
Stop anger go anger
Let us be happy forever

Stop anger, go anger
Keep moving keep moving
Stop anger go anger
Let us dance together

Stop anger, go anger
Keep laughing keep laughing
Stop anger go anger
Let us laugh together

Stop anger, go anger
Keep trying keep trying
Stop anger go anger
Let us relax together

Stop anger, go anger
Be patient be patient
Stop anger go anger
Let's be patient forever.

My Path (To Gain Your Pleasure)
O my Lord, love me
Have mercy on me, love me
I only rely on You
I only long for You (I only have loved for You)

Touch my heart, O Lord
Show me the way, O Lord
Guide me, O Lord
Have mercy on me

Move me
Only in Your Way
Show me the way
To gain Your pleasure

O my Lord, shower me
With Your love, with Your love
Grant me Your mercy
I only long for You (I only have loved for You)

Because of Him
Do not cry, do not grieve
Keep smiling in bitterness
Keep hoping, keep praying
Have faith in His salvation

Do not worry, do not doubt
Trust that God is with us
Keep walking, keep moving
He will be here with His salvation

Your love, my love are united because of Him
Your love, my love are connected because of Him
Your heart, my heart holds on together because of Him
You live, my life is happy because of Him.

About The Author
Nika Suwarsih is from Indonesia. She is the secretary of the Multicultural Women's Friendship Network in Springvale. The Network is organised by women to empower women, mums and kids. It also offers free activities, including yoga, aerobics, parenting skills and law, meditation, relaxation, laughter therapy, art and craft, self-care, as well as multicultural activities, dance and cooking classes. Nika is also active in and supports the Indonesian Women's Friendship Network as its project coordinator.

She is also active as a laughter therapy facilitator in Melbourne. Nika has completed diplomas in counselling and family intake and support work.

She performs as a singer at multicultural events and provides counselling to others in the community. She is also active in and supports the Dandenong CALD Mental Health Professional Network. Now she has joined World Writings, Victoria to learn and to write her story.

JAY AND BLACK CLOUD

SAEED AFROOZEH

A dedication

This story is dedicated to all the kids in the world who suffer from autism. I, the writer of this story, hope that one day all those kids who have this illness get better. I wish to see the smile of happiness on their parents' faces and to see them wipe away their tears of sadness forever and enjoy life and put everything they went through behind them. God bless us all.

The mare Blaze died giving birth to Black Cloud. On the night Black Cloud was born Jay spent every hour at Blaze's side. When she died, Jay held the horse in his arms and would not let go. Dad and mum tried with all their might to pull Jay away. For ten hours his parents struggled to make Jay let go so they could bury the horse. At last Jay became so tired he let go of his own accord. Blaze was buried with a toy Jay threw into the pit.

Now my story starts because Jay and the colt Black Cloud were never separated. Jay slept with Jay in an annex to the stable. Every second day Jay's parents put down fresh hay then spread his bedding on top. Black Cloud grew and grew as Jay fed him with a bottle and teat. At four months Black Cloud was a beautiful black colt with a shiny black fringe mane, which Jay combed every day. Wherever Jay went, the colt followed.

In the village Black Cloud helped himself to the choicest cucumbers, carrots, melons or anything else he could fit into his mouth. None of the shopkeepers objected because Jay was strange and yelled and screamed and created chaos if anyone interfered.

Every day they walked together until Jay got tired, then he jumped on the colt's back without saddle or rein, holding only the mane and Black Cloud galloped like thunder, as if they were one body and two souls.

Jay could not speak, used primitive noises to communicate with Black Cloud and the horse would nod his head up and down and his hooves scraped the ground as if he understood. Their communication was out of this world, beyond understanding.

When Jay saw aged villagers carrying heavy loads on their backs, he had Black Cloud carry either the load or the load and the elder from his village to the next. He and his horse became very popular.

If anything bad happened to Jay, Black Cloud galloped home and fetched his parents and led them back to Jay.

Once circus people came to the village. The performers stood on their horses' backs. Jay and Black Cloud joined in. The ringmaster objected, 'We are trying to do business here and you are getting in the way!' Black Cloud kicked the ringmaster. The ringmaster fell to the ground winded. The show stopped.

The village mayor who was watching the show stepped in, calming the crowd, and sent Jay away. Jay rode to his nearby hiding cave, his special escape for when he or Black Cloud got into trouble.

The ringmaster wanted to press charges. The mayor said, 'You can't press charges. You need to leave now. I will take responsibility for this incident if it goes to court'.

Jay liked to play with the kids in his village. If anyone pushed or shoved him or did not do what he wanted then Black Cloud would come and nudge that person away. Even the biggest boys had to watch out.

At dinnertime Jay's mother put out a bucket of water, a mixture of barley and hay for Black Cloud and a plate of food for Jay. Boy and horse always ate together and drank from the same bucket.

One day the villagers decided to beautify the entrance road to their settlement because in winter it turned to mud and slush.

They brought sand, stones and clay using mules, donkeys and horses to carry the material to the village. Black Cloud was the strongest horse and the villagers needed Black Cloud so they asked the mayor of the village to persuade Jay to lend Black Cloud. The mayor refused, saying Jay was a strange, sick boy and his family too poor to take him to a doctor or the faraway hospital. Only Black Cloud helped Jay and to use the horse for work was wrong. Without Black Cloud, Jay would be unmanageable. The village accepted this logic and built the road without Black Cloud.

Jay learned how to communicate with others. He coloured papers to represent his feelings. Red meant no, black anger, yellow: I am feeling okay; green was the colour of friendship; white of sleep; blue, hunger and thirst; brown, toilet; and grey, washing. When Jay coloured blue, he also rubbed his stomach to convey his meaning. If the person did not understand, Jay coloured black anger and shook his head and shouted aggressively without stopping until he got what he wanted. Everyone in the village knew the code and wanted to help and see Jay colour green and smile and show his happiness.

Jay's father Hassan and his mother Zahra were illiterate, untaught, superstitious peasants who thought God was punishing them for their past sins. They never talked about Jay. When they thought no one would see them, they cried quietly. No one ever saw them smile. They were alone and saw themselves as not good enough for this world, although they loved Jay.

In the Middle East the bride and groom do not see each other until the night of the marriage and the parents decide who they will marry. If parents discover their children have any relationship with someone from the opposite sex, they punish them. Girls get more housework; boys have to collect dry scrub from the desert as fuel. Jay's parents were childhood sweethearts before they married and believed they had broken God's rule and Jay was the result. It was their wickedness that had caused Jay's strange affliction. They were guilt-ridden and ashamed.

Zahra and Hassan promised each other on their wedding night to be better parents than their own and to give their children a better life, to educate them and secure a better future. This is the dream of any parent.

After Jay's first year, they understood he was not normal. He could not concentrate and they could not attract his attention. They took Jay to the medicine man who said Jay was consumed by demons and should be taken to the religious catacombs to purify his soul. They must take him to the tombs every night from midnight to before sunrise for three months. When they took him home they had to wash him with rosewater, dry him and put henna signs on his palms and the soles of his feet. This was to be repeated daily. His diet was restricted to vegetables because any animal product would invite the demons back. He had to drink sweetened water and dress only in white.

After three months his parents were in despair because there was no change, so they took him to a city doctor but he was not able to diagnose Jay's problem. With this, the parents gave up and left his life in the hands of destiny.

Zahra kept her mind off the problem of Jay by working very hard and Hassan left home early, worked the farm all day and came home late. After dinner they would pray until midnight or when they fell asleep from exhaustion. This was his life until Jay found Black Cloud.

One night Jay went missing. Zahra and Hassan waited for him until late, but he didn't come home. Now his parents, who spoke to no one before, cried and begged others to help them find him.

Because there was no electricity in the village, after sunset the only sources of light were candles and kerosene lamps. They did not have torches so the possibility of finding Jay was small. A couple of people volunteered to help Hassan look. They began with the hills and mountains around the village. The weather was windy and the lamps blew out. They were determined to find him because everyone loved him and wanted him safe. They always helped if they could. They walked through hills and mountains shouting his name and whistling to attract his attention but there was no response.

They searched for hours walking kilometre after kilometre. Then the villagers stopped and returned to the village, but Jay's father did not give up. He farewelled everyone at the entrance to the village saying, 'It is my duty as a father to find him, dead or alive. Thank you for your help, go and rest. I will see you later'.

Hassan went out again on foot with a broken heart. He cried and asked God to look after his sick son. 'Please don't let the vicious animals harm him. He is sick and has never sinned. All he does is done without an understanding of the consequences. Have mercy on me and my son. Please reunite us as soon as possible.'

After walking and walking, he was so tired he sat down under a tree and like that he fell asleep. When he opened his eyes it was almost noon. He drank some water from his canteen and washed his face. Feeling calmer, he thanked his God and began to walk again. On the way he saw prints of bare feet similar to Jay's with hoof marks alongside. It could have been someone else or Jay. He continued hoping.

Eventually he met a couple of horsemen in the distance and put his hand up to stop them. They stopped. Hassan looked dishevelled and overwrought. He asked if they had seen a boy of Jay's description with a horse. They said 'No, we have not'.

'My son is not well and cannot talk,' Hassan said, 'He disappeared yesterday and no one has seen him since. He always comes home before dark, but last night when he didn't show up I knew something was wrong. Since then I have been searching without luck. I cannot go home empty-handed because I cannot see his mother cry'.

'This is a desert and you may die of thirst or hunger or get lost,' one of the horsemen said. 'It would be better if you went back and got a horse or donkey to ride'.

'I will go back home and get my old work horse and take him and some food and search again. I will continue whatever happens even if it costs me my life.'

'What about your wife?' the horseman asked.

'She has food stored at home for the whole year and a small well I dug for water in the back yard. The people of the village will also care for her until I return. In our village we are like brothers and sisters and they will do anything they can to help.'

The horsemen had tears in their eyes. 'We will help you because you are a selfless man and do everything for your family. You look poor, but you have a big heart. Your wife and son are lucky to have you.'

'No,' Hassan said. 'I am the lucky one. My wife has never asked me for anything, not clothes, house, jewellery or furniture. Since we married until today, she has had only two sets of clothing and two pairs of shoes. She has patched over the patches and she has washed the shoes so often her toes come through. Even with her broken shoes she went to the river, broke the ice and did our washing and she had to walk for miles to get there and back. When she came home her hands and feet were purple with cold. She would then go straight to the kitchen and cook for us. She would cook the food in the smoke filled kitchen with watery eyes. So last night when she asked me to find her son, I could not refuse. She put her faith in me so I must find him.'

Touched, the first horseman allowed Hassan to ride behind him on his saddle and the three men returned to Hassan's village. When they arrived at the village Hassan thanked the men and ran to his house.

Zahra was sitting on the doorstep and asked, 'What happened? Did you find him?'

'No,' and before she could say anything else Hassan said, 'But I will. I need my horse and some food for the way'.

Zahra prepared the food and water and readied his horse. Hassan said, 'You are a good wife and have worked hard in my house and we have lived together for so long. We have never had any differences and I have appreciated that, but now I must leave and find Jay and bring him back. I will not return until I have found him. Be strong and wait for us. I don't know how long it will take—a day, a month or even a year. If I don't find him my life will be without meaning. I know you are with me in this whether good or bad. So be strong and confident. Don't doubt me. Ever'.

'I will not doubt you. Our love for each other is a bond between us. We are two souls in one body. Nothing will break that.'

Hassan got on the horse, looked at the sky and left.

The country was in political turmoil and people did not travel. Army and security people were everywhere. Hassan came to an army checkpoint surrounded by trees and a field behind. A military officer approached and asked where he was going. He said, 'I am looking for my lost son'. The officer warned 'You are in a war zone. There is a curfew both day and night I cannot let you go. You might get killed'.

'But I have to find my son,' Hassan pleaded.

The army officer took Hassan to an army tent and said, 'Stay here tonight and at sunrise you can travel the back roads away from this war zone'. The officer also collected money and food from other soldiers and gave it to Hassan for his journey and Hassan was grateful.

Hassan left at sunrise, travelled all day until he came to a small town. A townsman said he had seen Jay. 'He was here yesterday with his horse and a soldier took them without telling anyone where they were going.'

Hassan got very upset. 'Who was that soldier? My son is sick and cannot understand where he goes and what he does. I must find him, but my horse is old and I won't catch up with them. Please help me and give me a strong young horse. I will return him.'

The man said, 'If the village chairman gives his permission, your horse will be ready tomorrow morning. Come home with me, rest and we will talk to him'. The mayor agreed to lend Hassan a horse and he left early in the morning, very tired because he could not sleep from all his worrying.

As Hassan trotted along on the borrowed horse he stopped army trucks and tanks, asking if anyone had seen his son. Some said yes and others said no. They pointed out where he should go. Day after day he travelled. After another two days he arrived in a small village that was not far from a lake and someone said, 'They may have gone to the lakeshore to see the ships'. When Hassan got to the lake he saw Black Cloud but Jay was not there. Hassan said hello to Black Cloud and Black Cloud allowed Jay's father to ride him. Hassan said goodbye to his other horse and began asking everyone at the lake if they had seen Jay with a soldier. An old man said, 'I saw a soldier but not your son. The soldier will come back if you wait'. Hassan waited.

After a while a young soldier appeared. Hassan approached him and asked, 'Where is my son?' The soldier said 'Your son was not feeling well and I left him in a nearby village'. Hassan said, 'Let's go now I need to see him right away.'

It took two hours for Hassan, Black Cloud and the soldier to reach the village. By the time they arrived the army had evacuated because there was a possibility of a missile attack, and had divided the villagers between five different bunkers that were spread over six kilometres of land. There was a curfew and civilians were not allowed to pass. It was impossible to find Jay.

Hassan told the soldier, 'If anything happens to my son I will hold you responsible because you kidnapped him and his horse to get you where you wished to go. From here you are on your own and I will find a way to find my son'.

Hassan went back to the village to return the horse he had borrowed and the owner of the horse said to Hassan, 'Stay for a couple of days and rest, maybe the military situation might get a bit better and then you can go and look for your son. With the missile attack going on at the moment you might get killed'.

'No, I have no choice' Hassan replied. 'I must go and find him and take him back to his mother. I must make this a priority.'

They prepared food and water. Hassan took two hours rest and then left. On the way he passed several checkpoints. Each asked him questions and when they heard his story they passed him from post to post. This allowed him to search the different bunkers on the way. But there was no sign of Jay. Some thought Jay might be in another bunker. Hassan continued until the army said he had to stop. 'No civilians. From this point onward only military personnel can pass.'

Hassan said, 'But what will happen to my son. He cannot even talk. I must find him'.

The officer in charge replied, 'Impossible. You must stay here. The next bunker you are heading for has been bombarded throughout the night. Even army personnel are not allowed there. Go to the nearest bunker and hide. Don't take this horse with you. There is no place for an animal there. Everyone has let their animals go before they went into the bunker'.

Hassan said, 'I can't. This horse Black Cloud goes with me wherever I go'. The officer responded 'Are you crazy?' Hassan said, 'No, this horse is like my child and I love him as much as I love my son. We see him as part of our family, not an animal, and we treat him accordingly. My son's life depends on this horse's life'.

Tears came to the officer's eyes and he said, 'I don't want to argue with you. We are at war and I am trying to explain the situation to you'.

'Wherever I go this horse will go and if we die we die together, so be it. My son is gone. I won't let you take this horse from me even if it costs my life. I will find another way to do this.'

Hassan rode back with Black Cloud to the previous bunker. The officer in charge grew very angry. 'During these attacks many men, women and children are killed and you only think about your son. What makes you any different from anyone else? In war no one looks at who is sick or not, they kill them all and everyone tries to save his own life. I understand your position and I am sorry, but my job is to see you safely into the bunker and make sure you leave. You are the same as everyone else. Don't waste my time, just leave.' and he ordered a soldier to escort Hassan to a bunker and no matter how much Hassan begged, the soldier would not listen. The officer then grabbed Black Cloud from Hassan and watched the soldier march Hassan off and into the bunker. Then the officer let Black Cloud go.

Black Cloud remembered the way he had come and went back to the village they had left. When the villager who had spoken to Hassan saw Black Cloud, he took him to his house and tied him in the stable. Black Cloud did not want to stay and shook his head trying to communicate but the villager could not understand what the horse wanted. The villager decided to keep Black Cloud because if Hassan was alive he had to go this way to return home.

Hassan's bunker was overcrowded. There were at least sixty people squeezed into a very small space. Hassan could not breathe and he did not want to talk to anyone, so he just prayed and hoped to find his horse and son and go back home, and he refused water and food. The people in the bunker could do nothing to help Hassan, although they wanted him to feel comfortable.

At night Hassan did not sleep but paced about the small space silently or asked to be left alone. In the end they all decided he needed to leave and asked the guard to remove him from the bunker. He was taken back to the officer who said, 'You are making trouble for us here. I will send you to the central post and the colonel will decide what to do with you'.

Two soldiers accompanied him to the army headquarters and put him inside a cell. After two days the colonel decided to send him back to the village from which he had come.

Hassan refused. 'I can't go back. I need to find my son.'

'It is not up to you,' the colonel said. 'Early tomorrow morning you will be on your way back to the village. This is an order and you cannot disobey.'

Hassan's cell was dark, cold and tiny with not enough space to lie flat, and he had only one old rough army blanket to wrap himself in. At 6.30 in the morning a soldier came with a tray of breakfast and said, 'Eat this and get ready. We have to go because we have a long journey in front of us'.

Hassan said, 'I will not leave without my son and horse because I do not have anywhere to go and my life depends on him and his horse'.

With a bitter smile, the soldier said, 'This is an order. You have no choice. I ask you to kindly cooperate and don't make me use force because…' and he touched his gun and left. An hour later he came back. Hassan was sitting quietly in the corner of the cell.

The soldier said, 'Too bad for you haven't eaten but we must go'.

When Hassan resisted two other soldiers stepped in, handcuffing him, and put him in an army jeep. On the way he asked soldiers, 'Is it okay to pick up my son's horse?' At first they refused but because he insisted they agreed.

When they arrived at the village where Black Cloud was it was getting dark and the owner of the house told them the roads were not safe at night because of the war and that cars were not allowed to use lights. The soldiers decided to stay the night and would leave first thing next morning. The owner made them a big feast. When dinner was finished the owner, who knew Hassan's situation and that the soldiers wanted to take him back by force, told them, 'Look you are both young and without family and have no idea about a sick child, and cannot understand him. But by looking at him you can see he has not eaten for days or taken a shower or even shaved. Tonight he also did not eat dinner. He is killing himself bit by bit and no one would do that for no reason. Only God knows what is happening inside him. This man has done no one wrong. He has worked hard and provided for his family, but he holds himself responsible for his child and will not talk logically. People in such a situation are dedicated to their children for life and sometimes will give up on their other children. Now he has lost his only child and the situation is even worse. So he left his wife, his village and his life to find his boy and he wants to see it through to the end. So brothers, it is better for you to leave him with me. Stay a couple of days so your officer will not know. Just say to the officer that you dropped him back at home. I will see what I can do to help him find his son. I ask you to help him as human beings. Think about what I have said'. He then went and made them another cup of tea.

One soldier was almost persuaded but the other said, 'Are you crazy? Do you know in war if you don't obey your orders, you can face court martial? I understand he is in a bad situation but we are soldiers and have to obey orders. Right or wrong, that is what being in the army means. When you join you put yourself into the army's hands. For the two years of compulsory army training there are many things you may think of as wrong, but you have to carry out the orders. We will take him back to his village tomorrow morning. Do not listen to our host, we do not know his motives. He is asking us to do something against the law and he knows nothing about it. He has been a peasant all his life and speaks only from his emotions and not logic. I am tired and don't want tea and we have a long way to travel tomorrow. I am going to sleep and I suggest you do likewise'. He then went off to sleep.

The other soldier lit a cigarette and asked the peasant to explain the situation further so that he could think it through. The peasant said, 'Look young man, in this world each one of us has a reason to live which makes life easier for us. Life is not easy by itself and because you are young you may not have the experience that when a man and woman marry they promise to stick by each other in happiness and sadness, in sickness and health, and when a child is born their life gets even more committed and they will enjoy life more. They will be proud of the child's first step and the first word, and, as he grows and finally graduates, they will become even prouder. This is every parent's dream. They share these dreams each day. "If he is a boy we will do this, or if it is a girl, we will do that" and try to bring their child's wishes to fruition. If the child is malformed they will see this at birth, but the strangeness of his son Jay was something they only found out later, so all their dreams are suddenly lost. Their child is not normal; their child is different. They try to push this thought aside and hope for the best and that the condition will go away—until they reach acceptance. I cannot explain their pain. To accept the condition would bring their lives to an end. Their hopes are shattered into a thousand drops, like water hitting a rock, and there is no going back. It is a one-way street. To tell you the truth, when I met Hassan not so long ago I cried for him when I was alone and asked God to return his son. That is why I will do anything to help him. So what do you think now?'

The soldier listened so intently he burned his fingers on his cigarette and said with tears in his eyes, 'Leave this to me. I will talk to my mate and try to convince him. I cannot promise you anything. Now I need to sleep'.

The next morning when everyone awoke he said to his friend, 'Let's stay here for a couple of days and then return to Army Headquarters and say to the colonel that we dropped Hassan at his village. Nothing will happen. The owner of this house will help Hassan to find his son. Hassan has not committed any crime in my eyes. He only wants to be a good father'.

The other soldier said, 'No. I will not let him influence you. Our job is to take him and we will. There is nothing else to say'.

They had breakfast. Hassan had gone to sleep in the lounge. The first soldier tried to rouse him to eat but could not wake him. The first soldier turned to the second, 'You go and start the car and I will bring him'. The soldier was not able to start the car because the battery was flat and there was no mechanic in this village to fix the car.

It was a very awkward situation. Now the soldiers had to stay in the village and also because the war was close—they could hear the shooting—they had to stay put.

The first soldier was happy, but the other one's blood was boiling and he would not talk to anyone, only walked around the house muttering to himself, 'We will find a way out of here'.

The owner of the house said, 'If this situation continues we may not get provisions for up to a month. Not even kerosene for our lamps. We will then be rationed. There may even be a famine'.

The first soldier said, 'So we must stay here and cope like the others. We should not lose hope'.

The same night the host said to Hassan, 'Eat and rest, I will send you with a tracker at night. You can rest in the day and check our bunkers and villages by night. Perhaps you will find Jay. The soldiers are not familiar with this area and only know me so they will stay here. Tomorrow morning I will tell them you have left and I don't know where you are. They will not find you because they don't know this place'.

'I won't leave Black Cloud behind', Hassan said.

After a small argument the host agreed, 'Leave tonight. Keep it quiet when you go. The tracker knows everything. Go and do what he says so you are not killed or captured'.

When they left it was too dark to see but the tracker was good. They went through hills and mountains. They could see missile hits in the distance. They entered a village. It was almost daylight and the village had been hit by a missile a few days before and no one was there. They went into a house, hiding themselves, stayed till night then continued their journey.

They came to a bunker with thirty or forty people inside. No one knew about Jay. Hassan and the tracker continued their journey village to village, bunker to bunker, but no Jay.

Now they were almost at the front line. The tracker said, 'We cannot go any further. We need to go back or die. From here, it is just desert'. Hassan accepted this and they began to retreat—Hassan, the tracker and Black Cloud.

They passed many villages destroyed in the bombing. Hassan could not accept that his job was finished. 'I have to try everything and anything even though I am reliant on people for food and lodging for Black Cloud and me. I put my faith in God to lead me to my son. It is natural when all else fails to depend on God.' He prayed each day that God would keep his son safe. He promised God, 'Once you return my son, I will never lose him again. If I return empty handed my wife will despair. I cannot see her like that'.

The tracker tried to calm him. 'You are not alone in this world. Look at what is around you. These people have lost everything.'

But Hassan could not see beyond his own pain, his mind so full of Jay and said, 'I am very grateful to you and I may not be able to pay back your help, but please do not talk about my pain because, without suffering as I do, you cannot know my pain. Every day I am faced again with having lost my son and he wants to say something to me, but I cannot understand or help him. All I can do is cry out and eat myself from the inside. Every human being is born once and dies once, but I am faced with dying every day'. He sighed deeply along silence followed.

They arrived back in the village where they had met, to find it had been devastated by a rocket attack the previous night. Some villagers had left, but Hassan's host and his family hid in their basement and were still alive despite the devastation of their house. The tracker found that his house had been hit by a rocket and all his family were killed. He went into shock and fell to the ground. Hassan and his host pulled him inside and washed his face until he came back to his senses. The host said, 'Two hundred people were killed in the attack last night. Unfortunately your family was one of them but now all we can do is find their dead bodies and bury them and then come back and hide in my basement. Perhaps we will find a better place to hide than here. I have been waiting for you so that we could go on together. There is no hope here with our house destroyed. Shrapnel has wounded one of my cows. We will have to leave that one, take the rest and find somewhere safer. And we are running out of time before the enemy gets here'.

Hassan said, 'I am tired, the tracker is in shock. We need time to think'. The host brought some food. Hassan slept with Black Cloud in the stable believing that if there was another rocket attack, it was better to die with his son's beloved horse.

The tracker stared at the ceiling all night and could not sleep. The host put a blanket over him, closed the basement door and went to sleep with his family.

The next morning, Hassan told his host: 'You have helped me, but I must go. My destiny and yours are different. I cannot presume on your help anymore. I wish you all the best. Thank you.'

Outside, the village in ruins, he had no idea in which direction to travel: North, South, East or West. Everything was devastated by war. He mounted Black Cloud and rode until he saw army tents. He dismounted near the tents and approached the first tent on foot. He heard the groaning as he drew closer then he lifted the tent flap and saw corpses and three wounded soldiers. The soldiers asked for water. He gave them his water bottle and asked what had happened and where the other soldiers were.

One answered, 'Just leave, everyone is dead. If anyone returns, they will kill you too. You can do nothing for us. Leave.'

'I can't. I am looking for my son. If I die here it doesn't matter, but I must find him' Hassan said.

'Are you crazy, at this time, at this moment?' a soldier said. 'The enemy is everywhere. You will not be able to move, let alone find your son. You are insane'.

'Please tell me where the bunkers are. I must know,' Hassan said.

'There is only one way,' and he gave him his compass. 'Go east to the mountains. The gypsies live there. I am a gypsy, they might help you. It is a good four hours ride on a horse. Ask for a woman called Nargues, she is my mother. When you see her tell her Ali sent me. He was wounded in war and I could do nothing for him except give him some water before he died. He said you would help. Leave now because it is getting dark and you don't have much time.'

Hassan hugged the wounded soldiers goodbye and left. On the way he cried about his situation to Black Cloud. 'I came to find Jay, not to see all this killing, dying, bombing. There is nothing I can do for anyone. I must find Jay and return home as soon as I can.'

Hassan found Nargues after riding a long way. He left Black Cloud in front of her tent and ducked inside. Inside in one corner there was an old lady sitting on a carpet. She seemed to be blind. Hassan approached and said hello.

'What news do you have for me?'

Hassan told her about her son.

Nargues wept silently and then said, 'You are our guest. Please rest and have something to eat. We will talk tomorrow'. She told a woman to bring food, to water Black Cloud and fix a bed in an adjoining tent.

After supper Hassan went to the tent, lay down and slept. The rooster welcomed the day. Hassan woke up, washed his face and went to the main tent where many people were. They gave him tea and bread.

Nargues said, 'I think you are a very brave man to come all the way through war'.

'I have lost my son,' Hassan replied, 'and must find him. I will not return home until I find him. I am not as brave as you think I am, but even cowards become brave when something like this befalls them. There is no way but to fight and find my son, it is my only task'.

Everyone in the tent was drawn in by his story. One asked, 'How did your son get lost? It sounds like he is very young'.

Hassan said, 'Yes, he is young and he was lost almost a month ago and I have been looking ever since. I am tired of telling and retelling this story. I do not have the time, so please help me'.

Nargues agreed and provided a guide. Hassan, the guide and Black Cloud travelled north. On the way they were quiet. The guide dismounted now and then to find the shortest way. Hassan tried to converse with him, but the guide didn't respond so Hassan gave up trying. They heard missiles exploding, hitting, and felt the earth shake. The horses shuddered in fright. They had to dismount and calm them.

They came to an empty bunker and saw hundreds of spent bullet cartridges. This showed that people had been shot and the bodies removed. They rode on until it was nearly dark and discovered a village that had been hit by missiles some nights before. No one was there and there were no animals. The walls were blackened by mortar fire. The guide said, 'We will stay here tonight. This is safe because the enemy will not attack this village again'.

The next morning after a quick breakfast they continued searching. They met other horsemen on the road who said, 'Go back. It is bad ahead. People are looking for places to hide. There are enemy attacks almost every night. The bunkers are full and there is no space. The Red Cross tents are full of wounded people and the situation is bleak'.

Hassan said to the guide, 'Go, if you want to go back, but I will not return without my son even if I get killed'.

'I will come with you' the guide said.

They came to a bunker one kilometre from the front line. Inside the bunker were many children. The bunker was very hot and the children noisy. Hassan went to each child in turn, but Jay was not there.

'Who are you looking for?' an old man asked.

'My son, he has a mental condition and cannot talk.'

The old man said, 'I think he was among the wounded. Their tent is about half a kilometre from here. The doctors and nurses are there'.

'Wounded, my son is wounded. I will kill the enemy and burn their things to the ground.' He ran towards Black Cloud and jumped onto him.

The guide shouted, 'Wait, we need to do this the right way'.

Hassan did not listen and Black Cloud was galloping like thunder.

The guide could not catch up with them him yet he kept shouting, 'Wait, wait, we will get there. You might kill yourself. They will see your dust and shoot at you. Let us see your son alive. This is the border, they will see you!'

When they reached the tents Hassan jumped off Black Cloud. He checked the tents one by one for Jay. There was no sign of him. He kept asking the doctors and nurses if they had seen his son. All answered the same, 'People go missing during war. No one knows where they are.'

Hassan sat, his head in his hands, and began crying very loudly. A doctor who was a colonel came and asked what was going on. Hassan said, 'I am looking for my son. I don't know if he is wounded or missing. What should I do? Who can I ask for help? People are all in misery and fighting to stay alive. I don't know what to think any more or what to do'.

'Look Hassan' the colonel said, 'neither you nor anyone else at this moment can do anything except pray and stay positive. Do not talk yourself out of your search, keep going. When God opens the door no human can shut it. You can overcome any obstacle in life. Look for the potential in yourself. You cannot just let go and feel sorry for yourself. Every human being has a hidden truth within himself. This is confidence. So be positive, do not feel hopeless and pity for yourself. Use what you have and God will step in and you will feel prepared to accomplish what you want and to try to be more faithful to God. Do not give up. You have come to find your son. Believe in it and it will happen. Don't cry. The last thing anyone needs here is despair, because the only thing these people have is hope and you are taking that away by crying and moaning. I am in command and I order you to stop this nonsense at once or I shall keep you contained. You are not the only one in pain. Look around you, you selfish man. Do you see anyone in peace? If you think you are the only one who has lost his hope, then think again. You are tired, I will send you and your friend to another tent to eat and rest. So I will come and see you later'.

Hassan went with the guide and lay down in another tent. After a few hours the colonel came and said, 'Hassan you can stay here and wait for your son. In other tents there are people in similar situations. I cannot guarantee anything and do not want to lie, so I will leave the decision to you. The other option is that you can return home and give me your address. If I find your son, I will send him to you, I promise you. There is no third option. The choice is yours. You decide'.

When the colonel left Hassan told the guide, 'My friend, this is the end of the line, go back and tell Nargues I am grateful for everything your people have done for me, but I have to do this myself'.

'Are you sure that is what you want?' the guide asked.

'Yes, I am, so you can leave tomorrow morning.'

Next morning before the guide left Hassan said, 'I do not know what will happen here so please take Black Cloud to my wife and tell her that I love her, I always have, and I will stay here till I find Jay. My wife is alone. Black Cloud will give her hope until I find Jay. Tell her be strong and I will stay strong too. We are in this together, don't you dare doubt it'.

The guide agreed and rode away with Black Cloud.

After that day no one saw Hassan or Jay ever again.

For years and years Zahra and Black Cloud used to go and sit outside the village, waiting for Hassan and Jay to return for them, refusing to talk to anyone. The village people said Zahra went crazy, all the time talking to herself and crying. One day Black Cloud showed up alone at the village entrance. When the villagers went inside Zhara's house, they found Zahra lying down on a blanket atop the hay in the stable, not moving. She was dead and in her hand was a crumpled picture of her, Hassan, Jay and Black Cloud. The villagers put the picture on the gravestone in a frame to protect it from the sun and rain.

Twenty-four hours after her death, Black Cloud died. The community buried him at her side.

From that day onwards every week the villagers put flowers on both graves. Everyone in the village still talks about them all the time to keep their memory alive. Their house has become like a museum. Whenever anybody comes to the village, they visit the house and the villagers tell the story of Jay and Black Cloud.

We all die one day. The question is, whose name will stay alive? Jay, Hassan, Zhara and Black Cloud are names that will live forever and ever.

About The Author

Saeed Afroozeh is the eldest son born to middle class parents in Iran in 1963. His father was a teacher and his mother a housewife. At thirteen he left his country of birth, stayed in the homes of family friends and went to school for a time, first in England and then in Germany. His education was severely interrupted by the moves from country to country.

He came to Australia in 1993 and now lives in Melbourne. After spending many years travelling through war torn countries, Saeed's ability to watch closely and capture important detail enriches his stories. They reflect on history as it happened and the people it affected. Each story comes from his direct experiences in the dangerous places he travelled through on his perilous journey to Australia.

He wishes for young people that they learn from his stories that they should focus on their education and be careful to choose the right path. He hopes that others do not need to endure suffering in the way he has.

LIFE'S QUESTIONS, ITS PROBLEMS AND SOME ANSWERS

SARITA KUKLKARNI

In India when a girl is about twenty-two she is of marriageable age and her family starts stressing and wanting the girl married. We have arranged marriages in India, but there is a fine line between an arranged marriage and a forced marriage. In my family I was given freedom to choose, have some say in it. At sixteen, I was not keen to be married without having completed my education and wanted to have something to fall back on, just in case. I made this choice at the age of sixteen. This is the story I want to tell.

I was the eldest girl of an upper middle class family, my father's adored princess, and spoiled rotten. My father was a businessman, the breadwinner of our family and was like a godfather to our mixed family all living together in one house. At any time we had over forty people visiting in our house eating wonderful meals. We had servants who cleaned, washed and ironed fresh clothes for me to wear every day.

My father was a very busy man but always made time for his family and made sure everyone was taken care of. My father treated wealthy people and the very poor equally well. He had the gift of being able to make everyone feel important, loved and cared for. He was strict and wanted us to be well educated. He always said, 'Education is the one thing no one can steal from you'. We had to be in the top five rank in a class, and our class sizes were fifty to sixty students per section. We would never stand up, speak up or argue with him. I was sixteen when I first stood up to him, but he did not know what was happening then because he developed a fatal liver illness and had only months to live.

During this illness I became very close to him. In the last few months of his life, when I took my turn to nurse and care for him, we spent a lot of time talking about everything and anything. What he taught me shaped me as a person. His principles and his sayings became mine: *Never burn your bridges. Always be a giver rather than a taker. Respect everyone equally, without wondering how you can profit from him or her. Be true to your soul and you will sleep well. Parents are not there all the time, but your conscience will be. Put yourself in another person's shoes and imagine how they feel. It is easy to make friends, but hard to keep them.*

Living by his principles helped to keep our family alive and I have passed his wisdom onto my own children.

The night we cremated my dear father, I felt much older than my sixteen years and promised myself that I would never cry in public and never give in to self-pity. After his death things turned sour for my whole family. Living in a joint family without our father, and with a mother who had very little education and could not support us, meant we had to depend on our uncles and aunties to take care of us. It was not easy. Family politics were messy and upsetting without a leader at its head. I did not like to see my mother treated badly or abused. I made sure she was protected and cared for. There is a saying: *Harsh words create wounds that take a long time to heal.* We survived by adhering to father's ideals and through our faith in the Lord.

Dad's closest brother, my uncle, took his place during this crisis and took care of us. My dear uncle became the sole breadwinner with ten mouths to feed. He was responsible for clothing and educating us while attending to the needs of the guests who arrived nearly every day. He took care of us until we completed our education and began adult life. But all this time I wondered why my father had to die so young. He was only forty-nine, a good man who did everything right by the rules of our society, the universe and karmic theory, yet he was dead and our lives so changed.

The Indian society we belonged to did not appreciate our difficulties. It was a social taboo to accept work below our status. The petty politics of the joint family increased stress, and the fact that I was female presented various challenges. I stood up for myself and continued my education, because I did not want to marry young and have to depend on others for income, or risk becoming a burden to them in circumstances like my mother's. By the age of twenty I earned a Master of Science degree.

I wanted to continue with my studies but my family wanted to find a suitable match for me. I talked confidentially to my uncle asking him to support my desire to become a doctor—in those days we were able to take zoology as a major, yet qualify for entry into medicine. It was challenging, but I scored high enough to get into medicine. I was offered a place in the private university sector. I needed to sign a document accepting the place, then face an interview with a panel of academics.

Knowing my family could not afford the fees and additional expenses, I refused the offer. My very upset uncle and I quarrelled afterwards. He said he would do anything to help me to study medicine so I attended the interview despite turning down the initial offer. Fate, however, intervened. The six-member academic panel took turns questioning me not about academic matters, but focused instead on how I would cope supporting myself and finishing the course because they knew about my family; and my being of high caste did not help matters either.

I left the room with a heavy heart, sobbing and miserable because of the callous attitude of the panellists and because I had disappointed my uncle. When my seat was sold to the highest bidder, I felt life was unfair then paused to reconsider, and asked: is life supposed to be fair? No, I said, it isn't and I must adjust, accept life's challenge. So I revised my plans: I would finish my Masters in Zoology and then try to do medicine sometime in the future. I did try again to study medicine but the outcome was the same, so I accepted my fate and began work as a lecturer.

Now at twenty-two, society deemed it was time for me to marry. Marriage proposals, many from overseas, bounced back and forth between members of my family. The family started pressuring my mother, saying to her, 'Your daughter is older now. She should be married. Get her settled, and you will be free. Daughters are a burden'.

I felt compelled to bow to the pressures of their expectations and societal norms. We went groom shopping. The procedure is as follows: the prospective bride's parents send a photo of their daughter with her credentials to a mediator. These are passed on to the groom's family. Horoscopes are matched up and, if they like the photo and credentials, the groom's family invite the young woman and her family to visit them. If the would be groom's family decides that it likes the girl after meeting her, his family approach hers with its demands. If her family agrees to these conditions the marriage can take place.

Awful! I hated the process and threw tantrums. My uncle supported me, finding reasons to reject these many proposals. Unhappily for me, the suitor game of dismissing proposals could not continue for long. Pressure to make a choice came from every side. Yet still I did not want to marry someone I had only met once, and for a short time. But my family would say, 'This boy is right for you. His family is good'. Still I refused until my aunty said a cousin of hers from Singapore was coming to visit.

They had not seen each other for years. Everyone was excited about this visit except me. I cooked and cleaned while my aunty became anxious about what I should wear, and how soon I would be ready to meet this so called Prince Charming. Irritated, I ignored her fussing and continued with my own life. At last he arrived and stayed with us for a week. When he left he gave a letter to my uncle.

Our house had several bedrooms. One of them was a long way away from the others and easily seen from the road. We used this room for meetings and to discuss important decisions. I had gone out and, when I returned, I saw the family elders seated in our decision-making room. As I entered the house, my nanny said the elders were waiting and I must hurry and join them. I was immediately anxious, wondering what I had done wrong and in my racing heart, decided the elders were upset because I was rebellious and stubborn and had not accepted any marriage proposals. In the decision-making room I was given a proposal letter from the family of the man who had visited from Singapore. This was a different kind of marriage proposal. First, it was from a family my family knew well, and because he had spent a week with us I had had the opportunity to get to know this man from Singapore much better than the others. Everyone asked my opinion. I didn't know what to say; I was confused and realised his visit had been part of a family conspiracy to see me married. He had visited not just to see my aunty, but also to take a good look at me. I didn't know exactly what I wanted and needed time to decide.

New proposals kept arriving. I was fed up with this groom shopping and lost interest. I started to think perhaps Prince Charming was the one I wanted to marry. I told my uncle this, but he was unsure about my decision because after receiving his proposal letter we heard no more from Prince Charming—days became weeks, then months. Meanwhile others were pressuring my family for a decision. My uncle was torn between all the conflicting opinions. Eventually he gave in, saying, 'Dearest, we must go ahead with a different proposal'. This made me determined to marry Prince Charming, no matter what. I threw tantrums and was very upset because we had heard nothing from him, only silence since I read the proposal letter.

Despite feeling distressed I continued with my work and home life as usual. The college where I taught was huge, but had only one telephone located in the main administration building, together with a public address system. In the middle of my lecture my name was broadcast over the loudspeaker and a man entered the lecture theatre saying, 'Madam, there is a phone call for you. Come quickly. It is an overseas call'.

As usual I worried, unable to think why anyone would call at this time of the day unless it was an emergency and yet, how could it be an emergency when I didn't know anyone overseas?

I hurried to the phone, to find the entry and the corridor crowded with students, lecturers and others, all waiting to find out what this was about. Embarrassed and acutely aware of my audience, I picked up the phone and nearly fainted. It was Prince Charming. He asked me how I was and wished me a happy birthday. I had forgotten that it was my birthday. I finished the call and tried to leave but the crowd was excited, everyone talking and shouting about the overseas phone call. I hurried away from the crowd to walk in the fresh air to calm myself before returning to my class. When I returned to the lecture theatre, my name was broadcast again. I turned to wait for the office assistant to catch up. He handed me an envelope and when I asked what it was he said, 'madam, this is overseas mail and looks important.' Not knowing how to react, I blushed. I tipped him, and politely took the letter. Walking to my class I was unsure how I felt: embarrassed, yet happy too, because it was the first time that someone had written to me and confused because I didn't know what to expect from this joyful moment.

When I went home, I was prepared to tell the family elders about the incident at the college, but to my surprise as I came in, everyone made a fuss over me, looking at me in a weird way. My heart raced. Something must be wrong. What was it? What did they know? Prince Charming was uncertain if I would receive the letter he sent to the college, so he had sent another letter to my home. Now I had to say something and began: 'Kaka, (Uncle) I had a phone call today. And this letter came to the college.' The room went silent, waiting for me to tell them what happened. After I told them everything, I waited nervously for their response, but they asked me to leave the room and get on with my work as usual. I was puzzled by their reactions. Was it a good or bad thing? I went to my bedroom, and changed my clothes to begin my evening chores; my cousins surrounded me, worrying, smiling and cracking jokes, and trying to irritate me. I kept my composure and went into the kitchen where I could hear distant raised voices discussing my future: *How he can do this! What does he think? He has crossed the line! He should have accepted the proposal before this. Why did his elders not tell him, or us? What does he think? Where do we stand now? We must look after the girl's interests, she is our first daughter.'* It went on for hours.

I was happy, relieved. My prayers were answered; I was on top of the world, except . . . the elders were upset. I wondered what would happen now, and worried about the decision they would make. I had made my decision. My heart was set on Prince Charming. Once again life presented me with a situation for which I had no guidance. I could only wait and see what the elders decided, and then tell my uncle how I felt.

My darling uncle finally came in. He said everyone was upset and needed the situation clarified. Since the family had not heard back from the man, and the betrothal was not agreed to, his action in contacting me was inappropriate and had caused concern. He asked what I wanted to do. 'Whatever you think is right,' I replied shyly.

Uncle left. There were many phone calls back and forth and I could only hear one side of the conversation. Now I was upset and worried and when my uncle came into the kitchen he said, 'Prince Charming has not formally asked to marry you in his letter. We must see his family in person, so get ready. We will go tomorrow.'

My family's happiness and mine weighed heavily upon my uncle, and he opposed everyone else's opinions. I felt his distress, but I did not know how to ease it. I sought privacy and prayed, asking for answers. I wept silently into the night, missing my father more than ever.

Early the next morning I went to work and worried all day about my future. When it was time to go home, I was anxious. It felt as if the universe had conspired, but I did not know what it was planning for me, and I desperately wanted my future resolved.

We went to see 'Prince Charming's' family, only to find that his uncle too was undecided. Everyone was tense, upset, not knowing what to do for the best. If we called the suitor directly and asked him to confirm his proposal, it would be indiscrete.

On the other hand, we had other proposals to consider, and were being pressured to accept one of them. I was distraught with everyone, about everything. There was more heated discussion, and we had to leave.

At home, my uncle was impatient and troubled, but he supported me when the others all stood against him; yet, because of unyielding pressure from the others, he insisted I consider my other proposals. My heart was set on Prince Charming because: Better to marry to a person you know, than someone you don't. Further, Prince Charming was part of my extended family, and, if need be, the family would all get involved in helping us. My aunt, the Prince's cousin, decided to write to him; a discrete way out of the impasse. Prince Charming must confirm his proposal. In those days, we had to wait weeks to receive a reply by letter, so she sent a telegram. We received his response in a week:

'Proposal accepted as long as Sarita is happy to come and reside in Australia.'

Now I had to decide whether I wanted to spend the rest of my life in Australia. We accepted the proposal and notified Prince Charming. I was happy, but had mixed feelings about leaving home to live in Australia. I knew a few facts about Australia: it had a high incidence of skin cancer; its climate was cold; and there were few Indian people; the country had a notorious white supremacy policy and, as an Indian, I might become a second-class citizen. None of this mattered. The one thing that mattered was Prince Charming lived there. Also, I confess, it had been my dream to one day see the Great Barrier Reef.

A date was set and the elaborate weeklong celebration known as The Big Indian Wedding began with the families, distant relatives, known and unknown friends. Three thousand people attended my wedding on the day in July 1987 and my loving family prepared for it months before.

It has been twenty-eight years since we took our vows. Since then my husband and I have had many ups and downs, had our share of problems, joys, losses and gains. But when a situation arises like a cobra spreading its hood, setting off my questioning mind again, and I want to walk away from everything and say enough is enough, I stop and reflect on the past and feel the warmth rushing back into my heart. It is then I understand what is important and what really matters. I am strong as long as I have my husband beside me and hold onto my father's teachings and values. Everyone has their share of misfortunes, worries and setbacks. In the end it is worth the anguish of decision-making, so long as we communicate, try to understand and love each other, share, learn to patch things up and stand tall together to make something better than the situation we find ourselves in.

I look back to where I came from and where we now are and I say thank you to the universe. Thank you for guiding us, being there formed or formless, or in person and answering the questions, showing us the path.

I want to dedicate my story to my darling dad, aunty, uncle and to my mother. I want to thank my brothers, my sisters and everyone else who has been part of my life, directly or indirectly. They have helped to influence me and make me what I am today. Thank you, dad, for your values. I hope I have made you proud. I want to thank my husband for being so understanding, and being there for me through thick and thin, and for fathering my two lovely sons.

The lessons I want to offer are: (1) the foundation of a good relationship rests on knowing where you have come from and (2) value your relationships no matter what. Communication is the best tool to banish pride, ego and anger. Love should be the driving force.

Finally I'd like to thank Australia and the Australian people for making me feel at home. Until recently I used to say that India was home, but since my community work, I have felt at peace and at home more than when I worked in the corporate world. Thank you everyone for loving me, giving me strength when I need it and being there to support and walk with me. I truly feel that Australia is my home now. Lots of love to all and God bless you all. And stand by for my next exciting episode as a writer . . .

HOME TRUTHS

About The Author

Sarita Kulkarni arrived in Australia in 1987. I am an entomologist and agricultural scientist by profession. My favourite insect is the silkworm; I am fascinated by its silk production. I have worked in government and non-government sectors, and the corporate world. Since coming to Australia, I have worked as volunteer, helping newcomers and been a doula. I enjoy working with people, seeing them well settled and calling Australia their home.

Sharing one's inner life with strangers is a privilege; yet, when asked to write about my life, I wondered why share my story, and worried readers would not respect my attitudes and beliefs. Upon reflection I feel my story could be like a conversation, offering insights into my personality, my thinking and my environment.

Life on this earth does not come with a manual; yet, I feel as if I have been writing for a long time in my head, writing about being a woman, about pain and gain, about my lived experiences that shape who I am. I feel honoured to join this writing group, to be a writer, and share my positive experiences of solving real life problems.

IN DARKNESS AND IN LIGHT

THE FORGOTTEN PEOPLE ON EARTH: A TRUE STORY OF MY LIFE

WILLIAM DIMO

I was born in a suburb called Kor-ko (wrong-go) in Wau, the capital city of Western Bahr El Ghazal State, South Sudan, in 1972. Wau is in the north-west of South Sudan, on the western bank of the Jur River in Jur River County.

At the age of two I became very sick and my parents did not know what was causing my sickness, they believed it might be from witchcraft, perhaps from a lady who was jealous of my mother for having beautiful children. This lady was always talking to my mother about me, a few days after she said, 'You have a big boy and he looks handsome' I became sick. After I became sick my mother didn't think about taking me to the hospital because she assumed that my sickness was from the jealous lady who carried out magic which made me ill.

My right leg got swollen and very weak and I couldn't walk properly. The doctors did not determine what the problem was until I grew up and had some medical examinations. The results showed that it was polio. No one from my parents' generation knew about it, as at that time they believed in a traditional way of life; if a child is sick, they think what caused it was perhaps from a disgraced dead relative who had some differences with them in the past, or maybe from witchcraft.

Witchcraft is part of the traditional way of life and there are people who still practice it in villages. Parents would hide their children from witches because they were afraid the witches would kill them, just to make the parents feel the pain of losing a loved one. The witches could put stone, broken glass or green trees in the body of a child and if the child fell sick then the parents would have to go to the witch doctor to find out what was wrong. In my case I had polio, but no one knew about this sickness, so people thought it may have come from the witches.

My parents did try some hospital treatments but they had very limited knowledge about sickness. Doctors had limited experience in the 1970s, proper medical approaches were not known to local people and many died because of lack of education. Remarkably I survived the sickness which paralysed my right leg and walk using it, though I can feel it.

My father died when I was five years old and I was raised by my mother. Before my father died I learned a lot from his advice at his bedside when he was sick, telling me how I should live if he died. I remember all his advice. He told me that I was disabled in one leg; that I would not be able to do hard jobs so I needed to get an education and not just rely on my family. I should not think just about my family but think about education and this would help me in life. Even though I have siblings I am a son, so my life affected him deeply and I had to obey his wishes by going to school and studying.

He also warned me not to drink alcohol and if I did drink one day then I would see how bad it is and what disgrace and bad things would happen to me. A person who is kind, respects the elderly and follows their parents' advice will always have a blessed life. But a person who shows no respect and does bad things, for example adultery or stealing, will become disgraced and all their life will be cursed.

He asked me to swear not to drink at all. He also told me not to smoke cigarettes at all. He instructed me that I should give respect to all people whatever they looked like or where they came from.

He also said I should go and live with my cousin, whose name is Genaro S. Deng and who was raised by him, to get my education. I kept my father's wishes as he told me. To this day I have never tasted alcohol or smoked. The reasons for my father's demands not to drink or smoke gave me hope. I trusted him as I survived in the darkest days of my life, believing my father's soul was with me, guiding me as I kept his promises and not breaking one single word of his advice.

When I turned seven, my mother sent me to my cousin Genaro S. Deng who was a teacher at a boarding school in a small village called Mbili approximately twenty-four miles away from Wau city. It is a *Luo* tribal area in Bahr El Ghazal State and is also the homeland of my father.

In June 1978 I arrived in Mbili for the first time, the journey took nearly two hours due to a lot of rainfall, and for me it was a new life. We were welcomed by my cousin and given a place to sleep. The following morning my oldest brother George and I went for enrolment with my cousin. I remember the teacher who enrolled us; he was related to me as a cousin of my mum and his name was Gabriel Gog Mawein. I give the names in the story because in my tradition if I talk about someone without saying who that person is, no one will trust that I am telling the truth. The teacher explained the boarding rules and what uniforms we had to wear. I was enrolled in Grade 1 and my brother George in Grade 3.

In the boarding school we made many friends on the first day. The large rooms shown to us had nearly two hundred students sleeping in three big rooms. Students made their own bed from wood. Doors were locked and there were two adult monitors to observe children at night. If there was anything wrong, for example a child is sick during the night, the monitors had to inform the headmaster of the school or the teacher on night duty.

In all the rooms students had a can to wee in at night because no one was allowed to leave the rooms during the night. I asked one of my friends, his name was Uthoo Lonj, whose bed was close to mine, why we urinate in the cans. He replied, 'Lions are here in Mbili and they eat people.'

I stayed silent! 'Are you asleep?' he asked.

'No', I replied, and he then he asked me, 'Why have you been brought to study at a school in Mbili when Wau is a city where there are many schools?'

'My father wanted me to be where my cousin Genaro is, and my father told my mother before he died that I must come to study here in Mbili.'

'Okay, you need to follow your father's wishes or you will lose his good will,' he replied.

At that time, rain started falling and I heard something like a big crowed of people calling 'haeeeeo, a heeeyew.' It was hyenas, I started trembling, shaking and I said to my brother, 'We are dead, wild animals will eat us.' My brother was silent, perhaps he was also afraid. But my friend said, 'No, hyenas are not brave, only lions are, so do not be afraid.' I tried to sleep but I couldn't sleep from thinking about wild animals. Eventually I fell asleep. In the morning, the monitor rang the bell for the students to go out and get ready and to check attendance. All the students had to come out and line up so they could check how many were there.

The school bell rang and all the students, boarders and non-boarders, lined up in their different grades from one to six. I and my brother George were new arrivals. The teacher spoke and then the school principal welcomed us, all the students were clapping their hands and I was eager and very impressed, but the nightmare was still in my mind and I worried that my panic about the animals would come again in the evening.

I went to the classroom for the first day. I met many students and many were very kind to me. Then life began to become normal. I went to the bush to eat different fruits for the first time. I discovered that the Luo area has many trees which have good fruit.

The day lasted and nothing happened, also during the night I slept well with no nightmare. Life went on smoothly over days, months and years. I learned many new things and experienced many different stories that are still to be told.

In boarding school, students had no choice on what food they ate and water they drank. The food was bad and the water was unclean and, because of this, students sometimes became sick with malaria. Students were forced to eat any food the school provided. I remember one day at dinner, around seven o'clock, all the students sat in groups of five sharing from one plate. It was night and very dark and, because there was no electricity at all, students used firewood to give light.

While all the students were eating, one young boy sitting beside us told us that he thought there was something like lumps of yam mixed in the flour made from okra that had been mixed with dry meat and cooked to be eaten.

When the boy found these lumps like pieces of yam the other boys told him not to eat before he had looked to see what they were. But the boy went ahead and started eating and then he said, 'These things look like meat'. One of the boys near him said, 'Let's bring some firelight to see what it is'. When they brought the fire they found that it was a pregnant lizard. The boy started vomiting and then almost all the students in the school were vomiting as well. The students were not vomiting because of any poison but because it is not a good thing to eat a lizard.

I also vomited. On that day we slept without food and over the next three months I could not eat properly because there were insects in the flour and it smelled very bad—and the memory of the lizard did not help.

At the end of term one we had exams and when results came out I was the first student in my grade, with the highest score. The grade results for the top ten students in our school were called out and they got presents for their achievements. When the term holiday was over I started to love school because I was eager and proud. The gifts I received also encouraged me to proceed with my studies. But one thing was still in my mind—my father's advice before he died; that school is the only life for me, and he believed I would be a success. I kept my promises to my deceased father.

But there were still challenges ahead. The government in Sudan was discriminating against some citizens and denying them their human rights. People of Arab origin in the north were getting better schools, health and food than the people of African origin in Sudan. In Arabic the word 'Sudan' means black, and the Arabs who migrated to Sudan in the 1800's were in conflict with and created problems for the indigenous Africans who are the real people of Sudan.

The school I was studying in was built of mud brick with a grass roof. It was a temporary building not constructed by a proper builder. The four classes from grade three to six were under the school roof. The grade one and two classes were outside under the trees. We were lucky that in Mbili the trees are very big and provide very good shade. The students could sit underneath a tree without feeling hot sun on their heads or being in very bright light. There were no desks to write on. In grade one we used to write using our legs to support the paper and sit on local pieces of wood. The teachers used dusty chalk to write on the blackboard and this could make people sick.

A few months later, before Christmas, we had the same problem with food again. This time it was at lunch around three o'clock when one of the students found dry frog in the food. The food was dry fish cooked with *molokhai*, a sticky leaf that most Africans love to cook with either meat or dry fish. Putting some bicarbonate from a plant called *kombo* in this food can help to destroy any bad smell and perhaps also help to destroy bacteria in the dry fish. The boy took the frog, thinking it was a fish with its skin peeled off—scientists have warned not to eat the fish skin as it can contain poison. The boy started eating the frog thinking it was fish, but because it was very strong not soft and tender, he looked at it carefully and he said to the five students eating the meal with him, 'Look everyone, I have found a frog which looks like a fish', and all students who were eating in every group came to have a look. And suddenly, when they saw that it was a frog, some began vomiting and a small group of students became very angry with the cook because she was the same cooking lady who had cooked the lizard before.

I was lucky; we did not start eating because one of the students in our group was late after he went to the toilet to wash his hands. Before he returned the case of the frog in the food had become known and our group did not eat the lunch. When evening came all the students were trying to protest against the bad food, but the school principal intervened and spoke to the students to calm them down. He promised that he had already ordered cow meat to be delivered the next morning as compensation for the frog. Because of the expense it is difficult to afford fresh cow meat in Mbili. Most people can have it only once a month.

After the first South Sudanese war the government opened boarding schools: two secondary schools for girls and one primary school for both boys and girls. The boys in primary school have to go to another town, Wau, to go to secondary school. The Luo people did not like education for girls. Also parents send boys who they think are lazy to school. These are boys who are not active at home doing duties, like farm work or hunting, that are expected of young men. The parents think it would be better to send boys like that to school.

The local people are Luo people who have been given the nickname Jur Chol. But their original name, known in Mbili and other Luo areas in Western Bahr El Ghazal State, is Luo or Jo-Luo which means part of Luo. The Luo are in many countries and are part of one of the biggest tribes in Africa. The Luo people of South Sudan are also called Acholi and Lokoro in the Central Equatoria State in South Sudan; they are called Anuak or Sholok in the Upper Nile State of South Sudan; there are three groups of Luo called Jur Chol, Jur Chad and Blanda Boore, in Bahr El Ghazal State. As well as the Luo in South Sudan, there are also Luo in other countries. Barack Obama, the President of the United States, is of partial descent from the Luo in Kenya through his father. There are Luo in Uganda and Ethiopia who are called Anuak. In the Congo, Tanzania and Central Africa the Luo are called Alur. All the Luo speak one language but with different accents.

The Luo people of Mbili are very peaceful and they love working very hard on farms caring for cattle, sheep, goats and chickens. They also love hunting animals and making honey. They also make oil from a tree called the *lolos* and get bicarbonate to cook food by collecting the ash from burning the leaves of a tree called the *kombo*.

Life before the war was peaceful. I never witnessed any violence. People went to work on farms without fear. Life was simple. There were schools and hospitals, but while they were run at a high standard in some areas in the North, they were neglected in the South because the Government of Sudan discriminated against its black African and coloured Arab citizens. People from South Sudan who went to the capital city were deported because they were black and Christian. A minority who were in the capital city for work were registered and not allowed freedom of movement within the northern part of Sudan. But people in the South were united and there was freedom to move around all the cities of South Sudan without restriction. The country was divided by skin colour and also by culture and politics, with Muslim Arabs in the North, and Christian Africans in the South. Sharia Islamic laws applied to all South Sudanese in the North but not in the South. We, in South Sudan, were seen by the northerners as *Kafir* infidels. In South Sudan we saw them as invaders who wanted to change our way of life and loot our resources to build their cities.

The Luo of Wau were the first people in South Sudan to discover iron ore. In the ancient ages history tells that my forefathers used iron to make spears, axes, and many tools for fighting and hunting. But when the English colonials arrived in the 1800s they banned the Luo from producing iron in fear of the Luo being able to discover more weapons that could be used against the British Empire. During those times the British were the strongest nation on earth and had conquered the largest area of the world after the Roman Empire. They fought the Islamic world and defeated the Muslims in the Crusades.

The British did give iron to local people to make many different farming tools, but they banned the Luo from using local iron and also banned the Luo from coming to towns carrying with them any guns or spears.

I have met many girls who studied in Mbili and when I presented myself and said 'I am from Mbili', anyone from the Mbili Senior Secondary School or Mbili Girls Institute for teacher training was very impressed and excited to tell about their good memories of Mbili. They talked about the way of life there and of the stories of what happened to them through their studies in Mbili. Their life was full of stories too. They talked about their teenage years studying in the village of Mbili far away from their family and other stories about the Luo people clicked in their minds when we met. They talked about the lovely Luo people supporting them in their studies and giving them local Luo groundnuts, oil, and beans as well as cassava, sugarcane, honey, dura sorghum, sesame seeds, okra, *temleaka* plant leaves, *malukia* leaf, *kerkedea* leaf, sweet potatoes, and yams. Many Luo people gave them vegetables and fruit to support the students in their studies.

A lady called Suzan Sherilo is now here in Australia living in Oakleigh. When she met me and asked me where I came from and I told her I was from Mbili, she asked me if I remembered any stories about things that happened in Mbili. I told her about the girls getting hysteria sickness in the Mbili Girls Institute for teacher training, and the story about the pregnant girl from Mbili Senior Secondary School.

It had happened, once upon a time, that there was a lady who was studying in the Mbili Senior Secondary School. This lady had a relationship with a young man from a Luo village not far away from Mbili. They would meet in the bush, as girls were allowed to go out into the bush in the evening to do revision of their studies. From there a relationship started between the young girl student and the young Luo man. And it happened that she became pregnant from the young man. When she realised she was pregnant, she took a knife and cut her stomach open thinking she wanted to do an abortion because, if the school discovered that she was pregnant, she would be expelled. She went to the bathroom and cut herself on her stomach, trying to do an operation to take out the baby. The pain became severe, so she went back to her bed in the large room that was shared by about fifty or sixty other students. On her way back to her bed she left a trail of blood drops from the bathroom to the room. She lay down on her bed but fell unconscious. Some girls saw the drops of blood and followed them and when they reached her they found her in critical condition and they called the teachers for help. The teachers called the local nurse from the Mbili clinic to do first aid to stop the bleeding. When the bleeding was stopped the nurse referred her to the big hospital in Wau for possible surgery. The teachers tried to question her once she was able to talk about what had happened to her. She lied and said a man from the village had stabbed her with a spear and then tried to rape her, but she was trying to hide her pregnancy.

A duty teacher was sent to Wau hospital with her. The operation was carried out successfully and the lady survived and the baby was not harmed. The Wau police did an investigation to find out what had happened and the lady confessed that no one had attacked her but that she became pregnant from a boyfriend who was a young Luo villager. She had fallen in love with him because, even though the boarding school rules about relationships were very strict, it is a normal part of life for a young lady to be in love with someone. The school rules banned student relationships. Any sexual activities while studying at the school were viewed with zero tolerance. She was discharged from hospital and went back to Raja Province where her family lived. The teacher who went to Wau with her went back to Mbili and brought back the good news that the lady survived the surgery and that it had not been a rape. But the girl had broken the school rules and was dismissed from school, giving warning to other girls not to fall into the same situation.

I told Suzan Sherilo that I knew this story very well because I remembered all these stories very clearly. Also, I had met that lady in Raja Province in South Sudan in 1984, and she was working as a nurse in the Raja hospital. I was presented to her by another lady who studied in Mbili. Her name was Abuk. She was married to a security officer in Raja and she had got to know me when she was in Mbili. When Abuk introduced me to the lady, the lady said, 'Oh my God, Abuk, you brought another Luo here after what they did to me and stopped my schooling?'

I was scared as a young boy and was afraid of the lady, but she laughed and said, 'don't be scared, young boy, I am joking.' She hugged me and asked me if I knew her story and I replied yes I heard about you but I don't know you personally. And she told me that the baby was a boy and he was fine. I went back home and I was happy to have met her.

In Mbili there were no young men; when boys finished primary school they were transferred to a senior secondary school for bursary boys outside Wau City. The ladies can't find boyfriends and this is the reason that a lady will fall in love with a primitive villager; there are no educated young men in Mbili, they are all in the town of Wau. If they come back to Mbili during the school holidays, they find the girls are also on holiday too, so it is very hard to have boyfriends and the schools have banned relationships with any sexual activity; anyone caught in a relationship of that kind will be dismissed from school.

Hysteria sickness in the Mbili Girls Institute for teacher training was spotted when many students became sick. The sickness started when one lady started screaming for no reason and throwing herself on the floor and biting other students. At the time the teachers thought that the sickness could be from malaria, but all the malaria tests were negative. The disease was contagious as many girls suffered from the same sickness, and we witnessed many girls crying and taking off their clothes and yelling and scratching themselves. Other girls were trying to calm them down. The school was closed because of the disease spreading between students. Many girls were rushed to Wau hospital for treatment.

I asked one of the adult students what hysteria was and he replied that the girls suffered from hysteria because they had no boyfriends and the only medicine that might work is to allow them to go to their boyfriends. All these stories stuck in my mind and I always remember those days and am asking myself what it meant to be a girl without a boyfriend—

and the only answer I had was from the story I told before about the lady who was pregnant and tried to do an abortion by cutting herself.

After one month of forced holiday the school was opened and all the girls retuned to Mbili and their studies went on as normal like before the hysteria sickness.

In 1983 the government of Sudan announced the exportation of South Sudanese oil to Port Sudan, which angered South Sudanese politicians.

Students held big demonstrations in all the cities of South Sudan. In Wau, many students were killed during the protests. I was in Wau during those days. I was waiting with my oldest brother for transport to go back to Mbili after a short visit. We were at the Jur River Bridge with other passengers waiting for transport to Mbili. Suddenly students came running past us and I was confused about where to go. My brother said, 'It's a protest', and started running, leaving me behind because I couldn't run due to the polio I had in my leg as a child. I took refuge in a hospital very close to where I was. The police and army forces were everywhere.

Many students were shot dead at the scene. A policeman grabbed my arm and dragged me to the floor. A woman passing by cried out and said to the police, 'What are you doing with that young boy? He was not with the protesters'.

The police officer slapped me on my face and said, 'Go now or you are dead'.

I was trembling and shaking from fear of being shot like the students who were dead at the hospital gate. I was in shock from tear gas and crying with hopelessness. I went back home and I met my brother and he was safe at home. I found my mum quarrelling with my brother because he ran for his life and left me alone. When she saw me she started to cry with happiness. I told her how a woman saved my life from the brutality of the police and army forces. The evidence was clear from my face; the finger marks of the policemen who slapped me were still there.

In 1984 all the schools were closed in Mbili because of the war spreading across all South Sudanese cities.

I moved to Wau and went to an intermediate school called the Mbili Mboro Boys and Girls Intermediate School. The school had been named Mbili Mboro because two schools had been combined and moved to Wau City because of the war.

I was in first year or year seven. I kept getting the first student marks in all my exams and the school was proud of me. But the war distracted me when, in 1986 the government created militias from local people from the Fratit tribes to fight against the Dinka and Luo. It was Arab policy to create hatred between the local people so they would kill each other and reduce the population of the South Sudanese by ethnic cleansing. They gave guns and money to the militias, but the worst thing was that they wrote on the back of the tanks, 'Kill the Dinka and Jur who are Luo, but have sex with the Fratit'. And this was meant to say that none of the South Sudanese were any good. The Arabs just sat back as we killed ourselves like slaves fighting slaves.

I am from the Luo people who were the first group who went into the bush with the Dinka to fight the government of Sudan because of its bad policies. Every night many Dinka and Luo people were killed. Wau city was divided between the police and guerrilla fighters, with the majority from the Luo and Dinka groups; and the army, most of whom were Arab and supported by the militias. Wau West was held by the Fratit and Wau East was held by the Luo and Dinka. Anyone from the Dinka and Luo who went to the west at any time would be shot either by the army or militia. In a place called Loglogo, which was an area of Fratit suburbs, there were two very large bamboo trees. One was to put the heads of Dinka who had been killed, the other was for the heads of Luo. When Dinka were killed, the Fratit played music on drums for two days. When Luo were killed, they played for seven because they considered the Luo smarter than the Dinka and harder to kill. The Luo made better trophies.

I witnessed a mass grave where the police collected dead bodies every morning and buried them in one big hole. I saw a bulldozer digging the grave and trucks carrying bodies to dump them in the hole. Hyenas would come in the night and dig out the bodies to eat the human flesh. Sometimes they left parts of the bodies on the ground. The water smelled like human flesh had been thrown into it because Wau gets its water from underground holes. Those holes are seven metres deep.

I wrote in my exercise book about the night I saw one family of eleven people killed by the army near our house. They were laid out in rows and blood was running onto the street where people passed by. It was in August 1986. On that day the police launched a war against the army, which had turned its guns against civilians as well as the rebels, killing thousands of people.

The police went house to house pushing people out and telling them to cross the Jur River to survive the brutality of the Arab army and militias against the civilians.

I went with my mum and other siblings, under severe fire and shelling. One good thing was that many of the shells could not explode because they landed in the mud along the Jur. The police were very brave and stood firm to face the army forces and stop them from advancing toward the East where the Luo and Dinka were based. I saw that army soldiers who were trapped in police ambushes were killed and their bodies brought by police trucks to the Jur River where they were tied with stones and thrown in.

The river was full of water as it was August, which is the rainy season in South Sudan. We did manage to cross the river by boat after waiting in long queues and paying money to the man who owned the boat. There were many bodies there of people who had tried to swim across but had drowned.

We spent the night on the other side of the river bank; hunger and mosquitos were becoming a second set of enemies. No one worried about wild animals because they would be scared away by the big crowds of people.

Many families had left home without food. In the morning people in police uniforms came to where we were based and they said the Governor of the State, Mr Albino Acol had come to an agreement with General Mohamed Abu Groan, the head of the army in Wau. The agreement was that the army would not target civilians, and would let the civilians return home. We then went back, but starvation remained because the army stopped all goods coming from the North to our areas in East Wau and only allowed goods to come into the Fratit areas in the West. If you tried to cross from the East to go shopping in the West, you would be killed by the militia.

My mother decided to leave and take us to her sister's house in a place called Kuwajeana. We went there on foot, walking for two days because there was no transport during the war. Life was good in that village, there was plenty of food and the people were kind.

In October 1986 some of the army forces were going to Tonj, a city under government control with a military base.

The rebels had a plan to ambush and fight them on their way there. The rebels came to our village and arrested me and my 16 year old cousin, called Manual Lual, to carry a load of weapons. I was very young and was not able to run if there were any attacks by government forces. I was given a small box the size of a handbag, full with bullets, to carry. It was heavy. My neck was pushed in and my chest was burning like there was a fire inside it. My brain was getting swollen with pain like there were many nails in it. I started crying and a rebel man who spoke Dinka told me to shut up. He said, 'If you don't stop crying I will shoot you'.

A senior officer heard him and stopped. He asked the man what he said. The man did not reply. We reached the place where the rebels had prepared themselves for the ambush. The senior officer let me go and the man who arrested me got into trouble for taking a small boy who was a civilian to the frontline. I understood what they were talking about because I know the Dinka language. But I was racing against time to get away before the rebels fired the first warning shots. Thirty minutes later I heard a big bang like rain and lightning and a noise like a single guitar string going 'shew shew' above my head. It was bullets passing over me. My ears got blocked. I wondered if I could be a bird and fly, but I had no wings. I wanted to be strong without polio in my leg so I could run faster, but I could not change this and my running from death was a desire to survive. I thought it was the darkest day of my life. But it was just the beginning; the real darkest days were yet to come.

I went back home alone and I found my aunty and mother crying like when someone has died. 'I am alive I said to them', and just at that time my cousin Manual Lual suddenly arrived as well. The tears of sorrow turned to tears of happiness from our return to the family. But we saw there was death on the frontline as a group of rebels came past carrying their dead comrades. A silence had come over all the rebels and it was clear from their faces that a great man had been lost.

This happened in the land of our ancestors who we think have lived here for millions of years, though no one knows exactly how long.

The Arab *Jalaba*, who are half Arab and half African but who chose to be Arabs, do not care about the civilians or about political solutions to allow people to live in peace as one nation. They only care about the resources of South Sudan, such as oil, gold, diamonds, copper, uranium, thick water, equatorial trees, iron and the rich fertilised land that is good for farming. These resources do not occur in the North. If there was equality and all were equal before the law, rebels would not have taken up arms to fight the government. But negligence and marginalisation is the result of war.

The time 11pm on the eleventh of November 1986 is stuck in my mind forever. I was in the village where the rebels had increased their activities and were arresting young men and forcing them to join Sudan People's Liberation Army (SPLA). I had been asked by the SPLA commander in this area to be his writer. I was good at writing Arabic and had a little English too. My mother saw that it would be very dangerous if SPLA/M took me. She asked me to go back to the town to see whether the school was open. I left for Wau with my oldest brother, George, my cousin Made Lual and one young lady from our village called Ajongo Madut.

We started our journey from home at 3 am and we were close to Wau at 6 am after two days of walking.

My mother advised me and my brother to carry sticks and spears for self-defence against wild animals. I said to my mother that there would be no wild animals because they would be scared from the gun noises every day. We all laughed, but my mum sighed.

On the way we met many villagers coming from Wau. They said there were many complaints of looting from groups of rebels on the way. We stopped at a place called Bar-wol. Before the war it was like a bus stop for villagers travelling on the road. The sky was dark with clouds and it was 4 pm. Suddenly the November rain started falling. This is a time when the grasses drop seeds for the new rainy season.

Big winds and thunder and lightning struck the bush. We sat under mango trees. The young girl Aduwal had a sheet, she asked me to sit with her so we could shelter ourselves from the cool weather. The heavy rain stopped but it was still like a shower.

We started walking again around 10 pm so that we could get to Wau and spend the rest of the night there, then go to the check point in the morning.

We were walking in a line, the young girl Aduwal was first, I was second, my brother third, and my cousin, Made Lual, was the last in the line. The girl, Aduwal, in front of me was anxious. I saw her looking to the left and right. Then, in the Luo language, she said to me, 'Look on our left, I can see something with light like a torch. I believe it is a wild animal. A lion'.

'Are you sure?' I said.
'Yes, I am.'

I spoke to my brother in Arabic, and I told him we were in big trouble because we were walking with a lion.

'I don't think so,' he said. 'It might be a distant fire. There are houses on the riverbank there.'

'No my brother,' I said. 'You are wrong. It's a lion.'

The road was not far from the Jur riverbank. When the November rain pushes down the grass, the bush looks very clear and the eye can see into the distance.

My cousin said, 'what are you talking about?'

'They say we are being followed by lion on our left side,' said my brother. My cousin, the last in line, kept silent. As an adult she knew not to talk about it as it could make us very scared.

The lion came close and closer. I could hear the lion's stomach, *croorr croorr*, like when someone spends two days without food and wind and gas make noises in their belly.

My cousin told me to get a stick as there were trees everywhere in the big African jungle. But my mother's advice to carry sticks and spears came into my mind and my brother and I got out the ones we were carrying. Sometimes people are like prophets and know what can come in the future.

Perhaps one of us will be a big meal for the lion to night I was saying to myself from inside my heart.

My heartbeats were getting strong and faster. My hair stood on end whenever a leaf touched me. I felt like I was one of the walking dead. The lion moved and we could see it was not far away. It was ready to attack.

I started talking with a loud voice as my cousin told us not to be silent but to talk with powerful voices, like men.

I was praying first to God, my creator, and then to my father. 'Lord, what have I done wrong in this world? My father died when I was young, and now you give me to the lion. Why, God?' I kept praying as I said, 'To you, my biological father, where are your promises that I will be a successful person? I did not go against your will when you said not to drink alcohol or smoke. Also, I kept school in my mind. Today your two sons are going to die. Where is your name in this world father?' I put everything in the hands of my God and my father.

After I finished my prayer, the flood water in the river pushed a big, dry tree over near us on our right side. It made big sounds, like gunshots. It took around one minute to fall and the forest shook with the noise. The young girl, Aduwal, in front of me was confused, crying that we had been caught by the lion. I grabbed her in a big hug and said, 'Stop crying, the lion will think we are afraid and attack us'.

After a long silence we did not see the lion, it had disappeared in the bush.

We kept walking on the deserted road, crashing through the big dark mahogany trees that were planted by the British colonists and still exist in the bush. Many animals find the dense mahogany trees a good place to hide during the day. And in the night you can't see two meters left or right because of the darkness.

After we crossed through the deep, dark bush we heard a call from the dark grass and trees on our left. It was the voice of a lady saying, 'My children, my children, are you carrying a torch? I saw a light and I came over here' she said.

'Yes mum', I replied. 'Can you come out here mum?' In Africa, if any lady calls you her children, then you call her your mum and this is a normal form of respect by the local people for an adult.

My cousin said to me, 'You don't talk to someone you can't see. Maybe it is some forest Gods'.

'But she called in our Luo language', I said, 'so she is a person'. I was braver than my brother who did not like to talk very much.

The woman in the bush came out and greeted us. She had leprosy that affected her fingers which had been cut off. We told her we did not have a torch but that perhaps a lion that had tried to attack us might have run ahead to ambush us and saw her and her light. My cousin asked her where she was going and she said she was going to the village. She said she was with a group of people and that looters had attacked them and she had run off on her own. All people who were with her had separated in the bush. We told her to keep walking with us toward Wau, and that if we could get near Wau we would stay there until morning and the lion wouldn't attack people in the daylight. She agreed and we went together and reached a place called Bar Agwenwed that had a big space and was rocky and was the first place where bush fires had burned down the grass. We sat down to rest but I told the others to sit in a circle facing back to back so we could watch every direction for a lion attack.

The cocks crowed to show morning had come. We had some groundnut and water that we shared. We said goodbye to the woman who we met in the bush. We went to the checkpoint where soldiers and security guards stopped us to see what we were carrying. We carried nothing except food for my oldest sister in Wau.

When we reached home we slept the whole day as we had not been able to sleep or rest during the night because of the rain, the lion and the walking.

I was happy that we survived the lion attack. The following day I visited my father's grave. Tears came to my eyes and I was happy thinking and believing he saved my life with God's help. I believed it was a miracle. At the grave I said my prayer, 'I will never break your advice. Ever'. I said it on my father's grave.

I have dreams and dreams and dreams that a lion is attacking. And when I open my eyes, I am at home and it is nothing but a dream.

At night guns sounded and every day was a greeting of good night or goodbye because you could get shot at any time. Life was like an egg, it could be broken at any time. You could smell death everywhere and at any time you could be shot by snipers in broad daylight. A nightmare—as many houses had been burned down and women and children and the elderly couldn't escape because there were gunmen everywhere outside the houses. They leave you with no choice; you can either burn inside your house or run out where you may be shot.

On my return to Wau from Mbili village in November 1986 I stayed at the house of my cousin who is called Joseph Akol. I went back to school at Mbili Mboro Intermediate. I was in third year, the final year of intermediate school. I met my colleagues and there were only nineteen students left from the eight-six at the start of our study. Most of the rest had either migrated to neighbouring countries or been displaced to North Sudan. Some had gone to join the rebels, others were dead or no one knew about them.

I had been absent from school from August to November but the head master allowed me to continue.

We sat exams in February 1987 and after the exams, my cousin, who was an engineer, Joseph Akol, was transferred to Western Sudan. He said to me that he would take me to finish my schooling in Khartoum.

We left Wau to travel to Khartoum on trucks guarded by the army. My cousin had a best friend from Western Sudan who was a commander in the army forces. I was nervous because I didn't trust the government forces. But my cousin persuaded me and we took the journey of three weeks and reached Khartoum.

My cousin took me to another cousin living in Khartoum, his name was Robert Donato Deng. I stayed with them and I was enrolled in a school for displaced students called Imatong Senior Secondary School in Omdurman, where all classes were done in English.

I studied all my subjects in English. An international support organisation funded the schools for the displaced and gave each student 150 Sudanese pounds every month. I moved out from my cousin's house and lived with other friends, because my cousin had children and only one bed room and we couldn't fit in.

In 1992 I sat the Sudan School Certificate for the first time, but I did not continue because life was very difficult. The student fund of 150 pounds stopped because I finished secondary school. In 1992 I was enrolled at the Sudan University of Technology, but I deferred because the fees were very high. I went to study a Bachelor of Theological and Educational Studies at the Catholic college and graduated in 1997.

In Khartoum displaced children were not allowed to study with Arab children because of the government system, which was an Islamic fundamentalist movement against the South Sudanese. All Sudanese governments followed the same system; following the Arab way of doing things to make an Arab State. I saw that everything was totally different when I went for the first time to live in northern Sudan. The culture of a united country had changed to be about identity, tradition, religion and skin colour. I realised the war had made clear that there was something wrong with the system.

I knew how we were not equals before the law in our country after I was arrested in 1989. When I went with a recommendation from the school to get my birth certificate so I could prepare for the Sudan School Certificate final year, I went to the hospital to check if my name was there. The officer at reception asked me about my identity card. I gave him the school card and the recommendation from my school that I needed my birth certificate to enrol for my final year of study. I was called in and questioned by someone who said he was a security guard and that he had the power to arrest me and put me in jail—if I didn't tell the truth he would say that I was a rebel. The Khartoum government intimidated anyone from South Sudan who they thought was a rebel. I was surprised that the hospital had security guards; it was usually a place where anyone, even strangers, could find safety. I told him that I was a student. Then he called some men and they took me to a very dark room where I couldn't see anything. A man I could not see told me I was in the room for one thing. I had to say yes to his questions and if I kept saying no then I would be dead. He put a pistol to my head; I could feel it but not see it because the room was dark and had no windows. I was not afraid because this was normal to me. I had seen dead bodies before, I had witnessed a mass grave and I had survived a lion attack. I was saying to myself, *if I fear death, death will always follow me wherever I go*. I stood still and ready for whatever would come next.

The man asked me, 'Are you a rebel?'

I said no.

'Why you are here?'

'I am looking for my birth certificate'.

'Why, for what reason?'

'For the Sudan School Certificate examination'.

'Is this your country?'

'Yes,' I said. 'It is all our country, including you'.

He laughed, then he knocked my head and said, 'You Christian black South Sudanese are Kafir. You are fighting Muslims and we will win, slaves never become masters. Go outside and wait there.'

He was provoking me so that if I said anything back in retaliation I would be dead. But I was calm and went out to the reception. The lady there asked me where I was born. I said I was born in Wau in 1972 on the 18th of February. She said the doctor will give you a note to take to another office. I was called into the lighted room where the doctor was and was given a note that I took to another office where I was told to come back in one week for my birth certificate. One week later they gave me a certificate with an estimation of 01/01/1971 for my birthday. All my documents have this same date of birth.

Thousands of South Sudanese who came to the North without a birth certificate were issued a certificate with the date estimated as 01/01/– for any year.

The cold war was in all corners of North Sudan. In the streets of Khartoum you could be arrested by security guards at any time and disappear. Many South Sudanese people lost their life because the Government security forces targeted Africans from South Sudan, accusing them of being rebel supporters.

The worst was that they arrested both sexes—men were killed; women were intimidated, humiliated and raped. Many South Sudanese who couldn't escape to the bush were either displaced in Khartoum or became refugees in other neighbouring countries.

People in Khartoum were put in the desert areas outside the city in areas like Mayo, Umbada, Shegla, Ras Sheitan, Dar Salam, Jebel Aullia, and so on. Thankfully the Catholic Church fought to help these people and opened many schools for children.

The children were living in a very hot, sunny land with no trees. Peoples often died from hunger and sickness. Those who were able to work in Arab houses doing cleaning were given food as a salary just to survive. Many women got wine to sell and, if they were arrested, then they went to jail because Sharia law forbids alcohol.

In Khartoum there were a lot of secret jails where anyone from South Sudan who was seen as dangerous to Islamic security was assassinated.

There was a human mill near the prison in the suburb of Cober. If you were killed they put your body in the milling machine to grind it smooth, then pumped the human flesh directly into the Blue Nile River.

I had been in conflict with the security forces for almost all the time from 1987 to 2003, when I left Khartoum. It is a long and distressful story and if you think about it too much the brain has to stop and you may go crazy. Silence is the solution, I think.

After graduating, I was looking for a job. But I refused to work in any government office in which applicants, in particular men, were subjected to conversion to Islam.

In Sudan, a person who was Christian and worked with the government had to convert to Islam to keep their job. Their Christian names were kept but they took Islamic names so people would see them as Muslim and belonging to the Muslim community. Most of them had been stamped with an Islamic stamp which has written on it, in Arabic, no God only one God. This was to allow them to keep their position.

The Islamic government policy in Khartoum was to change the whole of Sudan to be a Muslim country like Saudi Arabia. But the continuing war of revenge in South Sudan made it difficult for Khartoum to achieve its goals.

I got a job as a school teacher at the missionary school Comboni of Gubba, and was later promoted to be school principal at Comboni primary school of Triah at St Joseph's parish in the Khartoum Catholic diocese.

As a Catholic I was doing compassionate work with the church and helping many students from being forcibly made to convert to Islam. This is not because I was against Islam, but I was against a government that wanted to force people to accept its religion. Even if they converted to Islam people were still treated as slaves. For example, the people in Darfur in Western Sudan, the people in the Nubba Mountains and the Blue Nile people from Angassna, are a majority of black Muslims, but they are still called slaves.

Genocide happened in Darfur. Nearly 400,000 people were murdered in Darfur and about 3 million died in South Sudan. The death rates are actually higher; no organisation is allowed to get information because it is all blocked by the government to cover up its atrocities and crimes against humanity committed in the name of Allah and in the name of Arab Muslims.

In Sudan, if you speak Arabic and are a Muslim, but are not an Arab, then no one recognises you in the system. They say an Arab Muslim is a person who has Arab blood flowing in his veins and speaks only Arabic and is a Muslim. These rules mean that whatever the people of Darfur or Nubba do, they will never become first class citizens in Sudan.

The South Sudanese, who fought the government from 1965 to 1972 and again from1983 to 2005—just for equality and to be equal among all as Sudanese regardless of religion or skin colour—got their independence in 2011 because the government in Khartoum did not allow black Christians to be in higher positions above Arab Muslims. Islamic laws would not accept that and it is the reason Khartoum agreed to let South Sudan separate.

I have many South Sudanese colleagues now here in Australia who worked with me as school teachers back in Sudan. People like Simon Manas T-Bash in Bendigo who knows how capable we were and well organised to face the government, through the Catholic Church. I was arrested many times—interrogated, mistreated, punished with lashes, faced starvation, I was forced to hear the loud music of Quran Al Karim, I had cold water poured on my body and was threatened with death—all because they wanted me to stop working as a teacher and to stop preaching in Khartoum, as they said it was the capital city of an Islamic country.

The government of Sudan expanded radical Islam and became associated with the big terrorists in the world like Carlos and Osama Bin Laden. Carlos is a French national wanted around the world because of terrorism. My friend who is a Sudanese working in Sudanese security, told me he knew about Carlos— who was handed to France by Sudanese authorities after Carlos refused to assassinate the SPLA/M leader, Dr John Garang, in Nairobi, Kenya, in a deal between Carlos and the government.

Osama bin Laden was in Sudan from 1994 to1998. The Americans bombed a chemical company in Khartoum in 1998. I believe the company belonged to the terrorist Osama Bin Laden. This proved that Sudan was one of the most dangerous countries on earth. The Government of Sudan became a threat to world stability. Egyptian president Mohamed Hosni Mubarak survived an assassination attempt in Ethiopia that was planned by the Sudanese government. Sudanese jihadists were involved in bloodshed in Algeria. Palestinian Hamas officials were in Sudan for training and smuggling weapons to Gaza with the help of Sudanese authorities. I got to know all this from one of my friends in security who told me whenever these things were done. He advised me to leave Sudan. He said to take his advice seriously. I trusted him when I saw that all the events that he said took place were true.

The US government finally turned its attention to Sudan. The forgotten people on earth were saved because of the US and, in particular, Mr George W. Bush. This man I love; he is my rescuer as well as the rescuer of many marginalised Sudanese people of black African origin fighting the government of Sudan and living in regions such as South Sudan, Darfur, Nubba Mountain and Blue Nile. Black Muslims, Christians, non-religious men and women, the elderly, children and young people were rescued by George W. Bush who pushed the West to find out what was going on in Africa. If George W. Bush had been in power in 1994

I think he would have intervened to help people in Rwanda escape from the genocide.

In Sudan many people were able to make their way to the US, Canada, Finland and Australia because of George W. Bush, the bravest man ever. Even though they say he went to war and let the economy fail during the global financial crises, for me, George W. Bush saved thousands of people who were victims of the brutality of government dictators such as: the Islamic radicals in Sudan led by Omer El Bashir; the dictator of Iraq, Sadam Hussein; and the Taliban militias in Afghanistan. In darkness no one can see the mountains. But in light you can look even further than the eye can see, beyond and behind the mountains. You can see the flying birds on top of the mountains and in the sky. It is freedom.

On October the 10th of 2003 I arrived by ferry boat from Helfa in Sudan, to Aswan in Egypt. I then went to Cairo with my family—my wife and four children. My nephew, called Francis Silvio Ajeing, was in Cairo and he welcomed me to stay with him. In Egypt life was not so bad. Only Egyptians who are poor are big threats to migrants. Everywhere you go you may get intimidated, and if you seek revenge you will find Egyptians on top of you like ants with a fly. So it is better to be quiet if you have been insulted. You cannot go to the police or ask for help if you are in trouble. Just try to get out of it, or you may be deported back to Sudan and face the death sentence. I have heard many stories of people who had their kidneys and organs taken by the Egyptians but no one can complain. I was always praying not to get sick, because if you go to hospital, you are dead. Remarkably, my family and I were healthy for one year and then we came to Australia.

I applied at the Australian embassy in Cairo for a protection visa. I sent my application to Australia and in three months I was called by the Australian Embassy. I was handed a letter for an interview. In the interview the lady, whose name I forgot, so I called her an angel, asked me about my children's dates of birth and what happened to my leg. She gave me a medical form and we all did our medical tests. After three months the result came out that we were negative for all sicknesses and I was accepted to come to Australia.

We arrived in Australia at Melbourne airport at 10 pm on 2 November 2004. The customs officers were very kind but very strict and asked many questions. It is a normal procedure when someone enters the country. It is the duty of security to check everything. I wasn't afraid of anything because I observed that I was greeted by them kindly and in a respectful and polite way. They said welcome to Australia. As well, I had no problem speaking English and so no interpreter was provided because I was communicating with the customs officers normally.

I was embarrassed when a lady officer checked one of our bags and found dry fish in it. She called another officer and they were asking me, 'What is this?'

I said, 'It's a dry fish, Sudanese like them and I am bringing it to give to Sudanese friends here in Australia. Someone in Egypt asked me to bring it for her close relative'. The customs officer explained what was allowed into the country and what was not. She took a sample and put it in a glass with chemicals to test it. She said the fish would be thrown out because it was carrying disease. I agreed and they took it away. Then we were allowed to go out, and we went.

We were welcomed by my sponsor Mr Mathew Silva and his friend Edward Gabriel Yakand, and many people from the Luo community in Melbourne who had worked very hard to lend me the money for tickets to come to Australia. I give my thanks to Mr Marko Urbano, Polino Mayom and Nicola Alesio.

Travelling from the airport to home it was raining, but arriving in a new place is like seeing the world for the first time. You could not sit without reading the place from the views in your eyes. I was looking and I could see the city like the kingdom of heaven. Beautiful buildings, bridges, trees and the land is green. Everything is well organised. We went to Mr Jeramiah Mawin's house for temporary accommodation. We were warmly welcomed; the night was quiet and we slept until morning.

Life in Australia is wonderful and happy. As citizens of this country, I and my wife and children pay loyalty and respect to the government and its people. It is my duty and responsibility to acknowledge former Prime Minister John Howard who accepted many Africans to be part of the Australian community.

There are many challenges in daily life for those who have English language problems. I had no problems with speaking English when we arrived in Australia. I enrolled in AMES, an organisation that helps refugees, to learn English but my English level was high and the AMES administration gave me volunteer work as an interpreter. My two children, six and eight years old, were enrolled in English language school. The other two were very young. My wife also went to AMES to learn English. Life was smooth and within nine months I got my driver's license. Everything in life was amazing: taking kids to school, shopping and visiting many friends. In the beginning my plan was to get a job, but my overseas qualifications were not recognized because Sudan does not honour the relevant international agreements. Sudan was once part of the Commonwealth but the new Islamic state changed everything; they hate the west and western education.

Another challenge was cultural barriers and the issue of identity, race and social wellbeing. Some Australians don't feel safe when they see black people, and that is a normal perception. A minority of Australians feel threatened by some African migrants but the government and most Australians do not feel that way. I have many white Australian friends now, we live together in our neighbourhood and we visit each other and their children are friends with my children and my wife also has many friends in the Australian community. We are feeling welcome here and it is not like where we came from in Sudan, where we possibly faced the death penalty because of the violation of human rights and genocide. In Sudan the police and government are corrupt and kill its citizens. The Australian government respects human dignity and human rights. Australian laws are strong and no one is above the law. I love Australia and its people and its democratic system and values. Many children of migrants get a good education and are healthy and secure and they are tomorrow's future. I know there are some politicians with Islamophobia who are against all migrants, but most migrants are innocent and there is no place for them to live that is better than Australia. I believe my children would have never found this beautiful life if we were overseas. Australia is a home to my family.

In Australia I have no enemies and my family lives a better life. When I left my homeland, South Sudan, I did not know there is a country that gives citizenship and makes sure everyone can live a simple life without intimidation and humiliation. My future lies in Australia.

I was in darkness in Sudan on my path from my homeland of Wau to Khartoum and Egypt. I lost many best friends and relatives, and my father died when I was young. Now I am in the light in a country which preserves my dignity, respects me, gives me support, allows my children to go to school and gives me a chance to regain my hope. I have been here in Australia for ten years, no one has said to me you are under arrest. No one says in the open that I am black or a Kafir. I go to the Catholic Church, St Patrick's Pakenham, and my kids go there for their Catholic education. I work at St Mary Primary School, as a school teacher aide. I drive a car. I live in a house. I never dreamed of this when I was in Sudan. I went to RMIT University and finished an Advanced Diploma of interpreting. I am also doing a Bachelor of International Studies at Victoria University, with the help of government subsidies.

Who would have imagined that I would find myself in Australia? But trusting your parents' advice and following what they say is a blessing everlasting. I promised my father and my father promised me. His soul guided me and guarded me and the Lord was behind me at every step.

About The Author

William Dimo is a South Sudanese Australian who migrated to Australia and arrived on 2 November 2004.

William called his story *In Darkness and In Light* to reflect two very distinct phases of his life. *In Darkness* describes the difficult times of his life in war and his hard life as a child living far away from his parents. *In Light* describes how William successfully survived hunger and starvation in the city of Wau.

The South Sudanese were a forgotten people. The world turned its back on them. William witnessed mass graves in Wau city in South Sudan. It was chaos and horror. This was William's daily life until he came to Australia.

THE STORY OF THREE

AJAK KWAI

(*Ajak says as background to her story*: 'As a Sudanese woman I grew up in a culture where no one was isolated. It is my tradition that we understand and support one another. There are also clear expectations of how we should live. Among those expectations are: each member of the community is to put others first; a man must say "I am interested in a relationship with you" before courtship; if a man marries more than one wife the family lives together in harmony; if the wives have issues they may argue, but this should not involve the children who are always shared as members of the family and are not a specific woman's children. These expectations are very different from expectations I have encountered in Australia, where these ideas may be seen as idiot acts because it is expected that each person should stand up for themselves because no one else will. It is a pity that the culture in Australia seldom allows for such graciousness; to a newcomer from a culture like mine, Aussie culture is seen not as racism, but simply as *bullying*.')

Amira arrived in the small Queensland town of Winton as a fresh-faced young hopeful, determined to make a new life in rural Australia. She had travelled halfway around the world from Africa for this new beginning.

Settling into the small Winton community, Amira found the people of her adopted country to be generally welcoming and tolerant. Amira befriended Michael, a single older man. He quickly became her closest and dearest friend. The sight of a younger African woman and an archetypal Australian man never seemed to raise more than eyebrows.

Michael was a few years older than Amira, but his young-at-heart attitude and their similar interests meant the two friends could enjoy each other's company without complications, control or interference. Their unspoken boundaries allowed for a pure and platonic friendship: long on conversation and short on drama.

Over the years Michael began to feel a deep affection for Amira. He admired her kind heart and her willingness to accept life. Reluctant to admit he was falling for her, Michael kept his feelings at arms-length. Unfortunately Amira never suspected Michael was in love with her and instead often encouraged Michael to see other women. To Amira Michael was a free spirit, drifting from one life situation to another. Coming from a different world, she did not think it her place as his friend to comment upon what he should or shouldn't do, or who he should love.

Michael was always full of ambitious ideas that eventually faded to nothing. Michael's attitude to life puzzled Amira, but Winton was a modest place and so their friendship too drifted along at a steady, unhurried pace.

Then one day Elizabeth arrived. Outgoing Michael befriended Elizabeth in much the same way as he had Amira: rapidly, comfortably and without objection. It didn't seem to bother him that Amira and Elizabeth were such different women. Amira was shy, softly spoken and courteous; Elizabeth brash, opinionated and self-seeking.

Amira was initially mystified by Michael's interest in Elizabeth, but assumed he was a man of many friends and tastes, and consequently Elizabeth had a rightful place in his collection. Elizabeth was not so generous: Amira should not be in Michael's collection of friends and she said so often and loudly. At first Michael defended his friendship with Amira, but Elizabeth liked getting her own way, so Michael gave in, often breaking dates with Amira to keep the peace. Amira tried hard not to mind, not wanting to be an obstacle to their budding romance and remained polite, non-judgemental and accommodating.

The citizens of Winton kept to themselves for the most part, but, as in any small town, stories, rumours and innuendo moved swiftly as one person, then another saw what was happening. Elizabeth wanted to be married and Michael was single and had a steady income. Despite his faults and foibles—'Who cares?' she thought—Michael should marry her. The only obstacle Elizabeth could see was Amira.

Elizabeth began questioning Amira about her intentions towards Michael, insinuating it was Amira who was trying to snare Michael into marriage. Increasingly Elizabeth peppered her conversations with snide racial inferences, as if clever Amira was stupid and could not see through Elizabeth's meanness.

Moving her plan along, Elizabeth asked Michael to move in with her; a suggestion Michael initially resisted, confiding to Amira how reluctant he was to share a house with Elizabeth because it was too much like commitment. Honest Amira replied he should do what he felt was the right thing, because how could she decide for him? Michael acknowledged her wisdom and his own feelings and remained living by himself.

Elizabeth did not take no for an answer. She pressed hard for Michael to move in, offering the promise of an uncomplicated partnership. Elizabeth's persistence wore Michael down and he agreed and moved in.

As the weeks passed with Michael safely tucked away at home, Elizabeth's dislike of Amira intensified and her venomous words increased. When Amira said, 'Anyone regardless of their upbringing, skin colour or social standing, should be offered the respect and dignity all human beings are entitled to.' Elizabeth sneered, mocking Amira, questioning if the African woman had any idea what her well-meaning words even meant.

Although Amira felt very uneasy she supported Michael in his decision to marry—he must follow his heart even if it meant marrying the sinister Elizabeth. And every time Amira thought what a bad person Elizabeth was, she took herself to task; she was too judgemental, too critical, too disapproving.

Now that their engagement was official, Elizabeth set about casting Amira out of Michael's life. At first Michael resisted, but he grew tired of arguing with his bride-to-be and gave in at about the same time as Amira decided to see less of them.

Elizabeth continued to treat Amira with contempt and spoke her racist views more openly, saying dark-skinned people were not as attractive as light-skinned. 'Who'd want to have an African for a wife she taunted?' With each barb Amira's heart contracted, but she never argued back because she knew there was beauty and ugliness in all races.

Michael and Elizabeth had two children within two years, which provided enough of a distraction from their day-to-day unhappiness to keep them together in one house. Amira and Michael occasionally met up for coffee and a chat, but it wasn't like before; and always Elizabeth's long dark shadow hovered between them.

Michael dissolved into despondency and despair and finally confessed that Elizabeth was a terribly controlling partner; their marriage was a mistake. Michael left Elizabeth.

Amira found it impossible to pick up the pieces of their splintered friendship. Their easy laughter was gone, their tender intimate conversation lost. They both felt it, and neither one felt inclined to analyse what had happened between them. Amira acknowledged to herself that their friendship had changed over the ensuing years—everything is affected by time: people, feelings, circumstances and the world around them.

Some people can make others feel powerless simply because of their skin colour. Why, she wondered, are there distinctions based on skin colour in human communities? To Amira, racism made absolutely no sense. Winton had been a nice place to live—quiet, unassuming. Why did Elizabeth want to create division and use bigotry just to get her way? Where does racism come from? Is it a result of a deep inborn fear? Or is racism born of ego, used to prove one is better than others?

In the quiet of her house Amira thinks about racism and bigotry a lot. She knows life is hard and full of conflict, after all she has had first-hand experience of wars and distrust. Life in Australia is full of different sorts of pressure and can wear people down. Sadly, some who appear confident and powerful are often anxious and take their insecurities out on others. She knows people often use racism as a cheap shot: to get ahead in situations, or to gain an advantage. It may not be because they hate a particular colour or race, but because it is easy to discredit or offend somebody this way.

Amira left Winton behind; she wanted a wider brighter world and relocated to a larger city in the country's west to pursue a job opportunity. She works at a local school and has made new, good friends. Still, she misses Michael. She misses their before-Elizabeth friendship; it was pure, there was trust. Now she carries in her mouth the bitter taste of bigotry and narrow-mindedness and wishes for the time before Elizabeth.

About The Author

Born in a small town called Bor in the Malakal Region of the Upper Nile, Ajak Kwai grew up in a musical family. Music is central to Ajak's way of life and intrinsic to her cultural heritage. The Sudanese civil war damaged her community during the 1990s and she had to flee to the Sudanese capital, Khartoum, before finally leaving the last of her family in 1992 to go to Egypt. In 1999, in her mid-twenties, Ajak was accepted into Australia under the Humanitarian Aid Program. She migrated to Hobart, Tasmania and joined the small Southern Sudanese community there.

Since 2002 Ajak has sung in Dinka, Arabic and English at various Australian festivals, including Byron Bay, Apollo Bay, National Folk Festival, Port Fairy and Melbourne International Festival. The songs she sings are very close to her heart, inspired by her continuing love and hopes for her homeland. 'I'm not a politician,' she says, 'but music can take your message places.'

To listen to her is to experience her world in all its colours, rhythms and mystery and leaves you in no doubt as to the depth and richness of her Dinka roots. Music is the vehicle for her stories of extraordinary life experiences as a refugee exiled from her home. Ajak and her songs take us on a deeply feminine and unique journey; from the Upper Nile, to gospel singing in Cairo, to Melbourne where she has successfully fused her African roots with the grassroots of Australian music—vibrant Afro-soul songs. She sings about freedom, peace, love and ... cows. Ajak's move to Melbourne has added new depth to her song writing talents. In 2008, Ajak revealed her magnificent vocal range in an album reflecting her new funky, raw Aussie/Sudanese sound to great acclaim.

I WAS A PROXY BRIDE

KALI PAXINOS

My name is Evangelia. I was 18 years old when I arrived in Melbourne Australia as a proxy bride. Let me tell you my story.

I was the fourth daughter born to a family of tobacco farmers in the north of Greece. I was born in 1934 and my parents were disappointed at having another girl. As I grew older, a familiar conversation in our home was about the money needed so the girls in our family could marry. Our mother was already sewing linen sheets and tablecloths that were to become part of our dowry. And so it was that we girls accepted that our lives would follow the culture and tradition of our parents.

We lived in a stone house built by our paternal great grandfather. He had inherited a small plot of land and planted tobacco. As each generation grew to adulthood, their sons would inherit the land and the girls were given a dowry when it was time for them to marry. After the marriage ceremony the girls left their family home and moved into their husband's family home to begin their married life.

For years my father cultivated his land so he could sell his tobacco for the highest price. He was well respected in the village and my mother taught us to respect him. His word was law.

I was five years old when WWII started, but our country was not invaded in the first few years so I had the opportunity to attend the local school for two years. At the end of that year the armies of Italy and Germany invaded our country.

My father became a soldier to defend his land and country. The village was devastated. The church lay in rubble, the school was burnt, the crops were ruined. Food was difficult to source;

our animals had been killed. My mother was always checking that all her girls were locked indoors. She was afraid that the enemy soldiers would invade her home and kidnap them. Many months passed before the enemy was defeated. Many of the village people had been killed and there was so much sadness and poverty. Life was unbearable.

After months of searching, our father was eventually found wounded and we became a family again. Any money saved before the war had now gone, and my father was still not strong enough to start farming again.

He had hardly recovered when a partisan civil war erupted. Tragically, friends and relatives took opposite sides in the conflict and many families were broken apart. Our prospects of marriage were now becoming difficult; not only could my parents not afford a dowry, but there was a shortage of young males left in the village and many families were divided by political ideology.

I was now a teenager and there was no hope that I could return to school. My sisters and I worked with our father on the farm and life was beginning to improve.

It was with great joy that my brother Dimitri was born. His arrival into the chaotic aftermath of the war was indeed the hope my parents had for a more secure future. 'He will inherit our land', my father would proudly say.

'What about us?' my sisters would ask.

'Things will improve and we will give you money for your dowries and you can marry good boys in the village', would be my father's reply.

But life takes unexpected turns and my life was to take a dramatic path. My elder sister was now engaged to the son of the local mayor, with all the protocols of the culture and religion of my country. My other two sisters learnt how to make clothes from a neighbour so that they had a skill to enable them to leave the village. They had plans to live with a relative in the capital city, Salonika, where there were prospects of employment.

Although we experienced much poverty, people of Greek background from America, Australia and Canada donated funds to repair our church, St Sotiros. A new priest was appointed and our people joined together for prayers and guidance. And so it was that the village community began to recover. However, I was anxious what my future would be. So many of the young men from our village had lost their lives during the war and others were leaving to seek work in the cities.

At the village centre groups of women were gathering and listening to the president of the village reading a paper. Next to him were Father Andreas and two strange men. They were representatives from the Australian Government. They explained that Australia was interested in increasing their population. New industries were starting and workers were needed. There were many opportunities in this new country.

The Greek Government had an agreement with Australia, on establishing a scheme to bring young women to the new country to marry single Greek men who had migrated earlier. It was to be a wholly funded program named, Proxy Brides. The idea was for the men to contact a person in authority, usually the village priest or mayor, and request information about the availability of girls who would be interested in this program. The men often knew families who had unmarried daughters in the village where they once lived. They sent relevant details including photos. If the girl agreed, her details were then sent to the prospective groom and a proxy marriage was performed.

The girls were excited by this idea. Many came from poor families and had few opportunities to marry, mostly because their parents could not afford the dowry. I was one of those girls willing to be a proxy bride.

At first my father was not very happy for me to be involved in this scheme, but I was determined to persuade him to agree. I filled out the forms and waited. Eventually a request came from Gerasimos. He had been born in our village but moved to a larger town when young. My father knew the family so, after some thought, he gave me his blessing and approved the idea of the proxy marriage. The appropriate papers arrived from Australia, including the photo. Gerasimos did look handsome and said he worked in a factory making car parts.

Father Andreas performed the rituals, which gave me permission to leave my village and parents and travel to Australia and marry the man I chose. There was no talk of a dowry but my parents gave me their blessing.

The day I left, all my relatives and friends came to the bus stop to say goodbye. They were all crying but nothing would stop me now. I was so excited. I was now 18 and could make my own decisions.

The boat was full of girls like me. We clung to our photos. There were some men on board, but most were destined to work in other places than Melbourne where I was going to get married.

We had a few lessons in English on board, but most of us were either sea sick or disinterested, all we wanted was to meet the man we were to marry and live happily ever after.

After four weeks of sea travel all the girls were clutching their meagre luggage at the rails of the boat. 'We'll be reaching Port Melbourne at about 11 am', the captain told us through the loud speaker. We held our photos, hands perspiring. What will I say to Gerasimos? Will he like me? The ship moved slowly towards the port. Lots of people were gathered. There were posters, banners of welcome. Lots of people with bunches of flowers.

'Who is Gerasimos?' I looked at the photo again and again. There were so many people. Was he here?

About The Author

Kali Paxinos was born in Australia. Her parents migrated from Greece. She was the eldest of three girls. Her family followed the traditions and culture of the Greek community. She was part of an arranged marriage to Tatsi Paxinos in 1947. It was a happy one and five children followed. She is an advocate for social and health issues on behalf of migrant communities.

A CULTURAL MISUNDERSTANDING

CLOVIS MWAMBA

These stories and fables all show what farcical misunderstandings can occur when you have a clash of cultures; be that city and country, modern and traditional, rich and poor, Western and African or parents and children.

Australia
'Welcome to a country where you will eat legless and headless chickens.'

This is how I was welcomed in Australia by a Congolese man when I arrived in this beautiful country. At first I was shocked to hear such a terse welcome from a Congolese man. The only explanation was that it was his sense of humour.

Later on I realised that he was right; here I can't rely on a chicken. I have to rely on my watch because I can't find a rooster to wake me up. Slaughterers have already chopped off their heads and legs then sent them into supermarkets, so this means I might never hear a rooster crowing in Australia.

In discovering my new country I learned a few rules to remember for the rest of my life.

Here in Australia, people share meals and drinks in restaurants; and yet each person pays their own bill. This is a lesson for me because, in Congo, if you invite people to a restaurant, you pay the bill.

Speaking of interaction, I visited an African immigrant woman on the 4th of August 2010. An earthquake had happened in New Zealand. We saw it on the news. People looted shops. The lady cracked up laughing as she viewed the footage. She said,

'I thought looting only occurred in poor countries but I've just been proven wrong'.

This reminded me about looting that occurred in Kinshasa many years ago. A woman tried to prevent a child from looting, because soldiers had been ordered to shoot .The child replied while running, 'It's okay mother, looting started in the Bible. Even God knows about it, and God will always forgive the poor'. The lady kept on warning the child of the danger of looting. The boy replied, *'Bango pe bazali bato, ata ndele bakolanda ngai!'* meaning, 'Those people are human too. One day they will die too'. This saying became popular. Now it comes to mean you are fearless of death.

Talking with other Africans I realise we all love to share our knowledge through sayings or proverbs. It's the older generations' knowledge, passed down through myths, tales, minerals, flora, fauna. They provide positive guidance in the community. An example of such a proverb is: 'Giving birth is joyful, but raising is a challenge.'

Talking to the wall

Lying on my bed, I'm reading letters sent from my family abroad. I'm very excited because it's the first time I'm getting letters from them.

Dear Brother

We are thankful for your ongoing financial support. The family is very proud of you. To avoid further annoyance by calling you at night asking you for money, we would like to ask you one thing: send us the machine that vomits money from the wall. We heard it operates 24/7 and can be found in every developed country. I believe it's called an ATM. On behalf of the family we are asking you, if possible, could you just send us the money-vomiting-machine so that we can depend on ourselves and won't bother you anymore? We promise we will look after it very carefully so that no thieves will put their hands on it.

Never forget where you come from and those left behind.

Take care and God bless you.

Hi Brother

It's me, Cizuzu, your only and favourite brother of all time. How are you? Hopefully you're fine. Did you find a wife there yet? If you do, let the first boy have my name. Anyway, I've got something on my mind that keeps me wondering and I would like some clarification. During our technology class regarding automobile vehicles, I remember our teacher talking about trains that were made of iron. After he finished talking I asked him, 'How could such huge machines move onto the road?' He said 'They run onto railways made in iron'. This time I asked 'How do they stop?'

My teacher took a deep breath and said, 'People wait for a signal before the train reaches the station. First, the driver jumps out through a window. His task is to pull a string that will let down a hill of stones, which will stop the train with a huge sound like thunder. Then, after it's completely stopped, travellers are safe to walk out the carriages to go to their destination'.

When I wanted to ask more questions he told me to ask him later. His excuse was 'We need to move on because there are many things to discuss'.

I am highly concerned as to whether the teacher is lying or not. I know that you live in the City of Melbourne. I was told that Flinders Street was one of your biggest stations. This means you would know better than us. I want to know how trains work and what is it like being in a train? I heard that travellers sit comfortably and eat, chat or read their books or newspapers. I also heard that you have people on megaphones saying 'Mind the red line. Stand still. Stand clear'. Is this true?

If the teacher lied to me the whole classroom is fooled. Those students will spread the lie to their relatives and friends. Those relatives and friends in turn will pass it on in the villages and elsewhere. Whole generations will be fed with lies. Now you see my worry. If you can tell me the truth then we can break the circle. Please help me. I'm very curious about this.

Can't wait to hear from you.

Hi Uncle

It's your most lovely and cute nephew who is writing to you. I have never seen a car. My father told me a story about '*Gari*' (Swahili word for car).

A long time ago, when my father was young, he and his friends went to the city. On their way they saw strange, small houses shaped into iron. These were called cars and they ran on large trails called roads. They were roaring like lions while passing.

'You have to get off the road and hide before the lights flash on you, otherwise you die', one of them said. Fearfully, my father and his friends hid and changed their minds about going to the city. Since this story was spread, no one has ever wanted to go to the city again. Here in the village, Father is a trusted witness.

But I'm not sure if it's true or not. I'm living with doubt about this story. At school we studied that cars are vehicles that don't kill people but carry people. The light is meant for lighting roads at night to have a clear view. I'm so confused, because I have two opposing stories and don't know which one is the truth. If you have knowledge about this—hopefully you do—please write to me to clear up my misunderstanding. By the way, the whole village is proud of you; not only because you look after us, but you learnt literacy and numeracy. Everyone wants to be like you.

Cheers.

I'm not a virgin anymore

The girl's parents were well off, so they had sent their daughter to a Western style city school that was quite culturally different to the traditional way of life. On her way home she was preparing to announce some great news to her parents. They were both present, chattering in the lounge room, when she burst in and started talking about not being a virgin anymore.

The girl didn't receive the response she was expecting. Her father rained down blames and insults on her mother for raising her so badly, her mother started crying and the daughter was completely confused. Clearly she shouldn't have told her parents her great news. At this she was going to be the cause of her parents' divorce.

'From now on,' her father said, 'we'll expect the worst. I suppose it's hardly surprising. You spend hours admiring yourself in mirrors and obsessing over fashion. Look at that red lipstick and thick make-up on your face! You lie that you're going to the library and then at nightfall are dropped back off by a friend'.

'Stop fighting', said the grandfather as he entered the lounge room. 'Tell me what is going on before I start thinking the worst myself.' In their tradition parents could not talk to their children about sex, so the grandparents were asked to do so.

'The worst has already been done and we are fixing it', snapped the father.

'Good, well I'd better start packing', the grandfather retorted.

The couple looked at him in confusion, then demanded he ask their daughter for her 'great news.' The grandfather took her hand. 'Darling, tell me the great news that made your parents mad.'

'Today at school, for the first time, we staged *I Am Not a Virgin Anymore.*'

'Was it a piece of theatre?' interrupted her parents in excitement.

'Leave us', replied the grandfather. 'Keep on shouting at each other.'

What relief. Everyone started laughing.

'We're sorry', the father told his daughter as the grandfather headed to his room.

What a wonderful afternoon spent in a family that has judged so quickly before hearing the full story!

The cassava that becomes a child

It was harvest time. At dawn a group of women went into the fields. One discovered a mound of soil and the earth cracked as a cassava plant developed. She exclaimed 'This is mine!'

In the forest the hunter makes this cry to prevent other hunters from claiming the game. The women, hearing this claim, went elsewhere in search of cassava. Using her small hoe the woman began to unearth the cassava tuber. She heard a complaint from under the ground: 'Do not hurt me! Do not hurt me!' She persisted and continued to dig. A large cassava tuber will provide much better flour—very, very white. She dreamed of returning to the village with her trophy. She would exhibit the beautiful specimen to her peers. After a few days she would go to the river to soak it. All the women in the village would die of envy. Her husband and children would be happy.

Filled with pride, she finished clearing the soil off the tuber. That cassava renewed its complaint: 'Do not touch me! Do not touch me! Cover me, quick! Cover me, I am cold!' The frightened woman hastily reburied the cassava tuber and went elsewhere to harvest.

Another woman approached with her small hoe. She too departed very quickly, exclaiming, 'A cassava who speaks! My ears did not deceive me! I am not delirious!' She would also reap elsewhere.

Then came a childless woman. She bowed first to thank the ancestors and God for having blessed the harvest. She began to dig and unearthed a cassava the size of a human thigh that filled her basket. Instead of crowing in delight she took the cassava to the village and placed it in her attic.

Late that night her husband awoke and said he heard a strange noise coming from the kitchen. 'Sounds like children having fun', he mumbled, but she continued to sleep.

At dawn she went to the kitchen to take the cassava to soak it in the river. Entering the kitchen she heard the cries of a baby. In her attic she discovered a beautiful baby girl. She took the baby in her arms, warmed the body and thanked the ancestors and God for giving her such a beautiful gift.

Since then, the woman started to give birth to many children.

I am not your mother

I am living in regional Victoria, and here people from my community usually pay a profound respect to my age and consult me as their elder. This evening, a newly arrived family called me urgently to their house.

Was it a matter of sickness? An attempt at robbery or an accident? I found their door open so that I could come straight in. When I did, both the parents and their kids were so agitated that they were standing up in the lounge room. I felt the anger in the air and invited them to be seated along with me in the cosy armchairs. The mother asked their kids to move away after bringing a soft drink on to the table. I guessed it was a conversation between adults only.

The parents politely declined to share with me the bottle of soda they would usually offer, because they had to first vent their resentment. The father said, 'We have to work with an Australian lady through our process of settlement. Earlier, she stood on our doorstep and looked straight in my eyes, as well as the eyes of my wife and our kids'. He paused. 'What did we do wrong for her to disrespect us? My wife and I couldn't understand why she rebuked our warm welcome in our home.'

Apparently the woman had said, 'I am not your mother, not even the grandmother to your children. My name is Jane. That's it. Do you understand?'

The father said to me, 'What did my wife and I do wrong by respectfully greeting her as our "mother"? Why did we deserve this rebuke in front of our children? I am a husband and a father—which means that culturally I am a role model. Never, he swore twice—unless my mother raises from the dead—will my kids call her "Jane". How disrespectful they will look. Shame on her. My kids will not imitate such a silly example, otherwise they will end up calling my visitors who are not of their age by their names. I would just as well introduce a venomous snake into my house. I would not like to see that lady anymore'.

I understood the way the old Australian lady had expressed her assertiveness, standing on the doorstep looking straight into their eyes; this would come across to this family as an attitude of disdain. To act this way in front of their children was rude and unbearable, and so the family felt humiliated. It denied that couple their social status as a responsible husband and wife.

The parents had not realised that their visitor also felt offended by their cultural African welcome to their house by abruptly calling her 'Mum'—which, biologically, she is not. Both the host family and their visitor were locked in a misunderstanding through a clash of cultures. I had to settle this matter, but how?

First I went to meet that volunteer, who felt as though she was an unofficial social worker to the new African family. I realised that she had felt that she had failed in her initial contact. She had left them with the promise of coming back another day. Together we talked deeply about the inadvertent misunderstanding that arose from this cross-culture incident. We talked about politeness and the way of expressing respect accordingly. I explained 'For African people, the most important social statuses are in terms of gender and generations. It goes beyond biological bonds, or even the colour of one's skin—yellow, red, white or black. Their cultural diagram crafts out four core social statuses: childhood, adulthood, old age and ancestor. And so any human must be treated accordingly.'

Those newly arrived are unaware of the Australian culture. They brought into this wonderful country their unique ways and were kindly and polite. I said to the woman, 'You also have been genuine by greeting the family in the Australian way…but do not say that'.

Jane replied 'Over here we do not see things as they do; we see things as we do them. I am their host. They made a long journey; they went through great hardship back home, even in the protected refugee camp. Now they end up resettled in my country. I am not their social worker but a charitable woman who thought the people around me might like some help. Australia is a multicultural country, but even so, people like us need to think out of the box. But it is so hard when you have grown older, especially when there is a language barrier'.

Jane felt sorry for her neighbours so the next day she went back to apologise. She wanted the kids to be present too, even though adults don't mix with children according to those four core social statuses.

Since then Jane has worked as a volunteer within the African community as their 'Aussie grandmother'. Her husband has joined her too. They fill the gap between parents and their kids, even dealing with culturally sensitive issues that grandparents back home had to. For instance, they ease tension between teenagers and their parents.

One afternoon Jane, who was with the family, urgently called me. What in the hell had happened now? I jumped in my car. Again the door was open. This time it was Jane's turn to complain about people from her own community.

'I was driving my car when school was over', she told me. 'I stopped on the road, the engine idling, and called out to Peter. An Australian driver stopped his car, got out and yelled, 'Why did you stop? Who is that boy to you? Do you know him?'

I replied 'I am his grandma. Look!' At this point, Peter came over and hugged her: 'Grandma!'

Jane smiled. 'The stranger drove off without uttering a word. Peter and I got into our car and here we are.'

My hidden name

'Today is my birthday but no one has noticed', Tresor complained sadly.

'How could anyone know when you spend all day in bed, locked up in your room?' said his grand-uncle Cyan. 'Why didn't you tell us yesterday, or this morning?'

Truthfully, Cyan couldn't even remember his own thirteen children's dates of birth. He scarcely celebrated birthdays. He knew his wife was born when the birth registration was set up by the colonial administration.

Older generations like Cyan's relied upon classes of age that coincided with the initiation rites that they underwent at adolescence. They'd stay in the bush for almost one year. He knew his rough age by locating himself within a range of generations—in term of 'more aged than' or 'less aged than' or by naming a predecessor, a peer or a successor. It could also be achieved by counting numbers of dry or wet seasons. To be accurate, Cyan knew that he had lived through seventy-six wet seasons. He was born when people hurried up harvesting crops within the short dry season, which refers to the thirteenth month of the lunar calendar, which is January. When he got married, when he was nineteen, his mother handed down to him a satchel containing nineteen grains of seasonal maize, which he then kept in a corner of his bedroom. Each year his wife fulfilled that duty as inherited from his mother. He proudly exhibits them at his wife's birthday.

To cheer Tresor up, Cyan's wife, Marigué, hired five girls in their neighbourhood to carry up the goods purchased in the afternoon market: a live chicken, a variety of meats—goat, lamb and beef—vegetables such as cassava leaves, amaranth and seasonal fruits. Her husband paid for alcohol, juice and the anniversary cake.

At nightfall, again Cyan knocked at Tresor's door and invited him into their lounge. When the young star arrived all the lights were turned off in the house. A gathering of relatives, friends and neighbours were around a large table dressed up in the middle of the room. They cheered him and chanted the French *'Bon Anniversaire'* in his honour.

The grand-nephew, ostensibly excited and proud, had to blow out twenty-one candles. When it was time to make his wish he stood beside his grand-uncle and said, 'I want to tell you who I really am, but don't be surprised or take it badly. From the cradle of civilisation, people lie over days, over weeks, over months, years and centuries. Jesus, who took away the sins of the world, encountered that lie on earth. He was crucified, resurrected and ascended to Heaven. Thereafter, people still lie on.

'People especially lie on their birthdays. After all, the idea of a birthday is just the heritage of our colonisers; a Western tradition—whereas the things we traditionally celebrate are first teeth, puberty, our first jobs. So we enjoy lying to each other on our "birthdays", like it's an in-joke without any consequences. Nobody trusts a thing you say on your birthday.

'But I do tell the truth on my birthday', said Tresor. 'That very day I told you the truth but unfortunately you didn't believe me.

My truth stood for a lie. My birthday was three days ago.'

Mouths fell open as astonished old men in the room shook their heads.

'What do you mean?' exclaimed the head of the household, staring at his grand-nephew.

'Repeat it!' added another relative, who could not believe his ears. 'I am about to walk out. Tell me we didn't buy all these things for nothing!'

Tresor kept on talking, paying no attention to what was being said. 'My birthday was three days ago,' he insisted. 'You know that it's that very day that in our country people are allowed to lie.

'But today,' he continued, 'it is different. I told you a lie that you believed.'

At this the young people in the room laughed and cheered. They realised Tresor had played a joke on the people in the room of their parents' age. In our culture you could not joke around with parents, it was like challenging authority. But it was okay if your grandparents were there, as they were more like your friends—and your parents would never dare challenge them.

'Don't feel upset or ashamed. People want to get lied to anyway. I was born wrapped in peoples' lies. My mother was stranded in the maternity ward feeling abandoned. Nobody visited her. Though sad, she was at least happy cuddling her baby boy. Yet outside people were lying through their teeth, "How could that bitch lie over her maternity, which is a sacred ancestral institution?"

'Yes, gossip spread, the idea that this lady from nowhere was living alone like a man in her apartment. It is true that my mother was settled as a single woman in the city. She had escaped the village to avoid stigmatisation by white priests and their hypocritical black parishioners. My father was the principal of their primary school. After paying her dowry according to custom, and while awaiting their Christian marriage, he fathered me.

"What a calamity!" exclaimed the priest they confessed to. "Both you and Jeanette have failed as role models in the village, acting like pagans." My parents were expelled from their Catholic school, and so my father reported that to another white priest who knew a lot about the indigenous culture and who pitied them.

"A secret made in the confessional should never be divulged", he said to my father. He discreetly organised my mother's transfer from the village to a public city school far away. There he found an apartment she settled in, and a white doctor to look after her.

'As usual, each morning my mother went out and came back after 3pm. One day on her way to school she felt unease in her womb. She immediately decided to consult the physician, who told her she already was in labour and had to remain in the hospital. That noon she gave birth to her first baby boy. People could not believe my mother's immediate delivery. She only was eight months pregnant and had never had morning sickness, so nobody at her home or work had realised she would give birth so soon. People did not believe she gave birth that day just as you did not accept my true birthday,' Tresor said. 'People lie a little bit every day, but I never do on my birthday, even though I was a liar right from my mother's womb. Even she had not expected to give birth a month before her due date. "Darling, you cheated me", she used to say, seriously or teasingly. "You incarnated the spirit of a lie in my womb."

'Since then, on my birthday, she lights a candle to humbly thank God for such a gracious gift. My wish tonight is that I will never stop telling lies, because both truth and lies profoundly shape my inner self, and are the substance of human nature. At least the subtle art of lying finds complicity amongst people for applause. Today for instance, like in politics, I lied and you cheered.

'But anyway', he concluded, 'it doesn't matter that I lied, because my mother has lit a candle and that clears away my sins and yours. Now you know all about my hidden name, the one that is my DNA: 'The First of April'.

'Let's share our wonderful birthday cake. God bless you!'

About The Author

I was born and grew up in eastern Congo from a working class family. Delightfully, I opted for a school career. After my graduation in Educational Sciences (1969), a Master in Psychology (1972) and an Aggregation in Psychology (1972), I became a teacher (1972), a principal (1975), then Chief of the Division of Education (1976) in the Western Kasai province.

At the end of the Cold War (1989), the wave of democracy and the need for radical change spread over Africa. I was elected as a representative in the political institutions, the Sovereign National Conference (1991-1992) and the High Council of the Republic - Parliament of Transition (1992-1997).

Advocating for social justice, human rights, democracy, the rule of law and good governance was a direct path to jail. I was harassed, abducted, tortured, relegated to secrecy and finally condemned to capital punishment (1998-1999). I escaped being executed in secrecy, as a result of pressure exerted by the press, by political parties, non-government human rights organisations and western embassies.

Taking refuge in Congo-Brazzaville I organised the clandestine opposition and the publication of its bulletins (2000 -2007). I landed in this wonderful country, Australia, in 2007 and worked as African Parenting Educator within the Congolese community. Retiring in 2014 I now write poetry and essays.

MENTORS

Ian Gilbert is now occupied full-time helping people write their memoirs, assisting people with writing speeches (mainly weddings) and editing. He volunteered for this project because of his conviction that everyone has a story worthy of recording, especially refugees who need the opportunity to relieve their trauma by telling their stories. Refugee stories are part of the continuously unfolding story of Australia.

Siobhan Kavanagh is a social worker and a beginning writer from Melbourne with an interest in cross-cultural practice and the impacts of migration. She currently works at the Brotherhood of St Laurence's Ecumenical Migration Centre as a Strategic Development Officer.

Gemma Mahadeo emigrated from the UK in 1988. Just before emigrating she spent a year in the Philippines, her mother's country. She is a Melbourne-based poet inspired by her father's storytelling in West Indian English and by her formal classical music training. She is fluent in French and Tagalog (Filipino).

Carolynne Morrison has always been a writer, and is the proud mother of four children and grandmother to three grandchildren. Until recently Carolynne was a Registered Division 1 Nurse, but has retired because of illness. Over her two years with the project she worked with five writers, who, because of the pressures of life, were unable to complete their stories. We may worry about paying the mortgage, but a hunting lion requires immediate action!

Steve Murray, after studying film in New York worked in television and film roles with Channels 7 and 10, SBS and Channel 31, and spent a year as Visual Effects Assistant on the Paramount feature film, *Charlotte's Web*. Steve works as a live video producer and editor and provides technical support for music and journalism colleges. His writing has appeared in the *Melbourne Herald Sun* and on travel sites, and he is an official blogger for the Carlton Football Club. He has been a writer on *Neighbours* and has two television pilots under consideration in Australia and the United States.

Jenny Norvick volunteers at the Brotherhood of St Laurence's Ecumenical Migration Centre. She assists refugees and asylum seekers to prepare resumes and find work, and provides support to local refugee women's organisations. She worked with Bol over a couple of years to help him get his story down on paper.

Jill Parris is a counselling psychologist who was a refugee. She believes that by telling stories people can share difficult history with others and heal in the process. She began encouraging refugees to write their stories some years ago; it is out of this process that World Writings was conceived.

Caroline Petit has published two novels: *The Fat Man's Daughter* and *Deep Night* with Soho Press, New York. Her short stories have appeared in Australian Love Stories; literary journals, including the *Asia Literary Review*, and been broadcast on Radio National Australia. She is currently completing her third novel.

David Sier is a volunteer at the Brotherhood of St Laurence's Ecumenical Migration Centre in Melbourne. He helps refugees and migrants, mainly from Africa, with English for study and for job and accommodation applications. As a result he has started to learn many things about the complexities facing governments and civil societies in Northeast Africa.

Meg Selman with degrees in TESOL and Applied Linguistics has 25 years training, editing and curriculum development experience together with academic editing and proofreading experience. She currently lives on the Far South Coast of NSW.

Tania Sheward is a journalist, producer and journalism educator and is passionate about impactful storytelling. She honed her writing skills at the BBC in London for a decade before moving to Melbourne where she now lives with her husband (and cat). She too helped Bol to tell his story.

Yannick Thoraval teaches professional writing at RMIT University in Melbourne. He previously worked as a Senior Communications Advisor/Speechwriter in the Victorian State Government Department of Premier and Cabinet within its Office of Multicultural Affairs and Citizenship. Yannick's first novel *The Current* was commended by judges of the Victorian Premier's Literary Awards. He is currently writing his second novel.

Jenny Valentish is a journalist who regularly contributes to left leaning newspapers. She is the former editor of the city guide *Time Out Melbourne* and author of the novel *Cherry Bomb*. Having emigrated from London in 2006, she now lives in the Victorian Goldfields.

www.ingramcontent.com/pod-product-compliance
Lightning Source LLC
Chambersburg PA
CBHW050535300426
44113CB00012B/2113